Third Edition

GREAT JOBS

FOR

Psychology Majors

Julie DeGalan & Stephen Lambert

McGraw·Hill

New York   Chicago   San Francisco   Lisbon   London   Madrid   Mexico City
Milan   New Delhi   San Juan   Seoul   Singapore   Sydney   Toronto

Library of Congress Cataloging-in-Publication Data

DeGalan, Julie.
   Great jobs for psychology majors / Julie DeGalan & Stephen Lambert.—3rd ed.
      p.   cm.
   Includes index.
   ISBN 0-07-145876-X (pbk. : alk. paper)
   1. Psychology—Vocational guidance.   I. Lambert, Stephen E.   II. Title.

   BF76.D44   2006
   150.23'73—dc22   2005054398

1 2 3 4 5 6 7 8 9 0   DOC/DOC   0 9 8 7 6

ISBN 0-07-145876-X

McGraw-Hill books are available at special quantity discounts to use as premiums and sales promotions, or for use in corporate training programs. For more information, please write to the Director of Special Sales, Professional Publishing, McGraw-Hill, Two Penn Plaza, New York, NY 10121-2298. Or contact your local bookstore.

This book is printed on acid-free paper.

To Byron, who is the most patient person alive, with love.

Contents

Acknowledgments

Writing this third edition of *Great Jobs for Psychology Majors* provided a wonderful opportunity to make a variety of updates and add new information for the reader.

We want to thank our colleagues at McGraw-Hill who were so helpful to and patient with us. Monica Bentley, we appreciate all your assistance and patience!

David Zehr of the Psychology Department at Plymouth State University provided extremely useful assistance and guidance during the revision of this book.

We also want to thank Kristen Michaud and Marsi Wisniewski for checking website addresses for us. Barbra Alan sparked creative changes that improved the book. Your positive attitudes are much appreciated

Introduction

Psychology: The Personalities Amid the Science

The opening chapters of your very first college psychology textbook were probably devoted to an appreciation of the principles and philosophical foundations of psychology and a brief survey of its history. You learned that psychology involves the study and understanding of how we think, feel, behave, perceive, and sense. And your ongoing studies helped you realize that psychology does indeed have a fascinating history. Some of the best historical reviews include biographies and even photographs and sketches of the pioneering women and men who carved a niche for this new science out of the disciplines of philosophy, anatomy and physiology, phrenology, biology, chemistry, and medicine. As a branch of study, psychology has a relatively short history. As a result, many of these personal histories of experimentation and brilliant discovery still have an immediacy and relevance to the discipline.

Until the nineteenth century, psychology was very much bound together with many other branches of science and theoretical exploration, most notably philosophy. So, the history of psychology began with an attempt to "self-define," to somehow separate itself from philosophy, anatomy, biology, and the other fields of investigation into what makes humans "click." It was during the nineteenth century that the work of incipient neurologists, oculists, physicists, and physiologists began to accumulate data and results that truly belonged to the new realm of psychology and not these other disciplines. A good example of this is the early work of German experimenters, such as Ernst Weber and Gustav Fechner, that began as investigations into ocular perception and discrimination and then led to an early understanding that we all appreciate and perceive differently.

The early French contributions were medically, rather than physiologically, oriented. Through extensive documentation and observation of incarcerated or institutionalized cases, the French were singularly responsible for the early work in psychology that helped us to understand mental illness, especially schizophrenia. Differences in symptoms and severity of cases were noted and analyzed, and the beginnings of a diagnostic model were laid down. Although psychology was not part of medical training as an independent course of investigation, by the early days of the nineteenth century, most informed physicians were at least aware of the practice of hypnosis and the possibilities it held for understanding and treating mental illness.

All of this early work in the 1800s began with an emphasis on understanding our physical senses: how we hear, see, and even taste. This led directly to an understanding of our mental faculties: how we perceive, discriminate, learn, and remember. Slowly, out of this physiological background, came increased understanding of the human mind and both individual behavior and group functioning. New careers for psychologists were created as psychology changed in form, structure, content, and methodology.

Your textbook chapter that summarizes the brief history of psychology would require as much discussion of the personalities and identities of the early psychologists and how they viewed and labeled their own careers or life work, as of the content of the work itself. As individuals moved ahead in their own work and theoretical development, it became clear that psychology was a science of many, many subspecialties. During these formative years, psychology was often defined by its personalities—Sigmund Freud, Carl Jung, and Karen Horney, just to name a few—or focused on the major psychological perspectives—structuralism, functionalism, psychoanalysis, behaviorism, Gestalt psychology, and humanistic psychology.

The Psychological Perspectives

The first half of the twentieth century saw the development of a number of perspectives in psychology. These were centered around strong, influential personalities whose writings and work attracted much popular attention. Even among the general public, the names of Erich Fromm, Freud, Jung, Horney, Alfred Adler, Viktor Frankl, and Abraham Maslow are well known, though their beliefs about psychology may not be as clear to the person on the street. Many people know the perspectives by name, as well, though it might be hard for them to match the founding or important personalities with their perspectives. The most familiar psychological perspectives are discussed here.

Structuralism

This approach, which arose in the late nineteenth century, tried to identify the component elements of the mind and determine how those elements interacted. Edward Titchener, an Englishman who introduced structuralism to the United States, believed that there were three basic mental elements: images, feelings, and sensations. One of the most notable contributions of structuralism was research that analyzed tastes. All tastes are mixtures of the four basic tastes of sweet, sour, salty, and bitter. Structuralism eventually declined because it was limited to laboratory experiments and it relied on introspection, which studied only conscious mental experience.

Functionalism

Developed in the late 1800s, functionalism placed less emphasis on mental processing and more on the outcomes of that mental activity. William James, an American and the most prominent functionalist, studied how people act in the world, rather than in the laboratory. Other early functionalists researched how psychology could be applied to education, industry, and even to film criticism. James's legacy to psychology is a theory of emotion that is still used today.

Psychoanalysis

The perspective known as psychoanalysis is now completely absorbed into the mainstream of American culture. The concept of the unconscious, the significance of dreams, the importance and presence of conflict within our minds, and how that conflict affects our everyday life was the work of pioneers such as Freud, Adler, and Jung. They saw indications of dysfunction in all people, neuroses and behaviors that may not be healthy but do not prevent individuals from maintaining appropriateness in their lives. For these pioneers and the perspective of psychoanalysis, there is a continuum of human experience—from what is termed "healthy" to what is considered "mentally ill"—that is seamless and subtle.

Behaviorism

Behaviorism, a perspective that dominated the discipline of psychology for half a century, was built on the belief that observable behavior should be the stuff of psychological research. B. F. Skinner, the leading behaviorist of the second half of the twentieth century, stressed the consequences of behavior rather than stimuli. Behaviorism is still a force in psychology today, but its influence has declined a bit because it ignores mental processes.

Gestalt Psychology

This psychological perspective began with discoveries about perceptions of motion and movement. Perhaps you've participated in experiments where, in a darkened room, you wave a colored fluorescent light "wand" rapidly back and forth in the air in front of you. You will actually see a "screen of light" against which it is possible to project a slide image. That image appears against this colored wall of moving light as you keep your wand in motion. Some of what you see is memory. The rapid movement of the colored wand and how you perceive the trail of light that it leaves is related to synergy; this concept of synergy has added to the understanding of learning, perception, and other areas of psychology.

Humanistic Psychology

Maslow, Carl Rogers, Horney, and Fromm are members of a group of psychologists termed "humanistic," a reaction away from the clinical approach of the psychoanalysts. This group emphasizes the importance of culture and interpersonal relations in personality formation. It also describes the need to move toward an ideal self; to improve; to become better; to have richer, more connected experiences; and to self-actualize as the person we feel we can be.

Contemporary Psychological Perspectives

Three influential perspectives have come to bear in the last few decades—the cognitive perspective, the biopsychological perspective, and the social-cultural perspective. With their addition, the field of psychology has become even more diverse.

Cognitivism

This perspective combines certain aspects of Gestalt psychology and behaviorism. Work in psychology behavior labs studying the mental development of children illustrates many of the important theories of cognitivists such as Jean Piaget. This perspective has been deeply influenced by the computer revolution—researchers such as Herbert Simon began studying the human brain as a type of information processor.

Biopsychological Perspective

Heredity, the brain, and the hormone system are studied to determine their effects on psychological functions in the biopsychological perspective. Behavioral genetics and evolutionary psychology are included.

Social-Cultural Perspective

Psychologists working in this perspective question whether the research findings based on work done in Europe and North America are applicable to all cultures. Various cultures have different standards in terms of what is normal or what is desirable. Harry Triandis, one of the founders of this perspective, believes that we should view each culture as having adapted to a particular economic niche.

The Field of Study and Areas of Concentration

The world of psychology is one of incredible diversity that can sometimes create confusion in the minds of the general public, especially in the area of careers. When we use the word *psychology* in everyday language, the context is often the abnormal, the aberrant, or the inappropriate in human behavior and motivation. We use many words with *psycho-* interchangeably: *psychology, psychiatrist, psychoanalysis, psychotic*. The airwaves are filled with personality psychologists who diagnose or provide counseling on television or the radio. Many of these experts have Ph.D.s and M.D.s, but are equally as skilled in self-marketing.

Though these public personalities have some of the most visible psychology careers, they truly represent only the tip of the iceberg. Tens of thousands of others work far more quietly and effectively in schools, clinics, private practice, research laboratories, industry, medicine, and higher education. Using any of the popular search engines, a Web search on any area of concentration listed below will dramatically illustrate that field of inquiry. Consider the following career fields:

- **Clinical psychology.** Professionals in this field assess and treat people who exhibit mental or emotional disorders ranging from the expected repercussions of everyday life to extreme pathological conditions.
- **Community psychology.** How we function at home, at school, in our communities (neighborhoods, housing units, or group homes) is the province of this specialty, much of whose work is preventative.
- **Counseling psychology.** Helping people cope, make important and everyday decisions, and adjust to the stresses and strains of life through interpersonal dialogue and a variety of treatment therapies are the domain of counseling psychology.
- **Developmental psychology.** Human development, from birth to death, is examined in this specialty. Developmental psychology describes, measures,

and explains age-related changes in behavior in terms of individual differences and universal traits.

• **Educational psychology.** This research-oriented branch of psychology studies how people learn. It has important applications in schools, industry, and our ever-changing technological society.

• **Environmental psychology.** Advancing theory through research to understand and to improve interactions between human behavior and the physical environment—both built and natural—is the goal of environmental psychology. Architectural design, management of scarce natural resources, and effects of extreme environments on personality and behavior are some of the varied interests represented by this field.

• **Experimental psychology.** This much broader grouping of specialists, through research, studies basic behavioral processes including how people talk as well as understand and apply what they know. Research involving animals is often involved as a step in understanding human behavior.

• **Family psychology.** This relatively new field is concerned with the importance of the family as a formative structure in our lives. The prevention and treatment of marital and family problems through research and application includes a subspecialty in the prevention and treatment of sexual dysfunction.

• **Forensic psychology.** As we become more aware of the devastating effects of crime on communities and victims, we can appreciate a branch of psychology that assists law enforcement agencies in criminal investigations by analyzing crime evidence.

• **Health psychology.** Smoking, weight gain and loss, stress management, fitness, and even dental care can have major psychological implications. This specialty is concerned with the contribution of psychology to health maintenance.

• **Organizational psychology.** We spend much of our lives employed and this branch of psychology studies our relationship to work. Job productivity, development, enhancement, career counseling, retirement planning, job variety, and cross-training are all part of this branch of psychology.

• **Physiological psychology.** Behavior changes as a function of drug use, how brain cells function, or the genetic roots of psychiatric disorders are studied in this concentration. Most positions are found in academic settings.

• **Psychology of aging.** Understanding the physical, biological, sociological, and psychological impact of aging helps us cope with the catabolic processes of growing old.

• **Psychology of gender.** The development of gender identity, the impact of socialization on that self-identity, issues of abuse (both sexual and physical), and hormonal influences are all worthy of a separate branch of psychological study.

- **Psychometrics.** A strong background in math and data analysis is necessary for work in this area, which focuses on psychological testing and assessment. Private research firms, testing companies, colleges and universities, and government agencies employ psychometrists.
- **Rehabilitation psychology.** The effects of birth trauma, stroke, or other debilitating handicaps are remedied in part by the work of rehabilitation psychologists who help people overcome situational and psychological obstacles to improve functioning in the world.
- **School psychology.** School psychologists assist with the emotional, psychological, and intellectual development of young people. Employed by educational systems, they counsel, work with children experiencing problems, collaborate with guidance personnel and teachers, and deliver workshops and programs on educational issues.
- **Social psychology.** Why are different female body types in fashion? Why does a culture revere young people? Which jobs have organizational status? All are subjects for social psychologists who are interested in our attitudes and opinions and how they are formed and changed.

New careers continue to appear as additional areas of concentration emerge. Expressive therapy, for example, has strong psychodynamic roots and psychologists such as James Hillman have been instrumental in forging new careers, especially for art therapists.

Current Issues in Psychology

As in any science, but perhaps more so in psychology where the number of possible presenting issues are infinite, controversies solved are quickly replaced by new ones. The use of antidepressants to treat depression in children, couples therapy, the continuing intrusion of politics into the health-care system, overcoming terror, and the tracking of child molesters are just a few of today's issues. The psychological community grapples with these issues in the press and at scholarly and scientific congresses.

A study completed by the National Institute of Mental Health (NIMH) outlines the growing prominence of mental illness as a leading cause of disability in major market economies such as the United States. Major depression ranked second only to ischemic heart disease in magnitude of disease burden in established market economies. Schizophrenia, bipolar disorder, obsessive-compulsive disorder, panic disorder, and post-traumatic stress disorder also contributed significantly to the total burden of illness attributable to mental disorders. Our understanding of mental health is becoming increasingly more sophisticated and with that growing understanding come increased opportunities for therapists, preprofessionals, and other employment categories in the areas related to psychology.

Molecular and cellular psychopathologies studies seek to understand the neuroscience of psychopathology at a molecular and/or cellular level; its goal is to reveal how direct and/or indirect alterations of molecular pathways lead to symptoms or symptom complexes that are characteristic of mental disorders. Just as the psychoanalysts saw a continuum of mental health, disagreement exists on what constitutes abnormal behavior or thinking. If the norms are socially determined, then psychopathology becomes an outgrowth of social enculturation—a response to society and what it believes is healthy and not a science unto itself.

Controversies continue about the best treatment for adolescents with depression—the use of antidepressants versus talk therapy or some combination. Concerns have been raised that the use of antidepressant medications may induce suicidal behavior in youths.

Where Do Psychology Graduates Fit Now?

In the most recent past, psychology graduates on the undergraduate level seeking employment have had to make do with jobs that overly generalized their skills from psychology to simply "people" skills. Graduates were not directly using their training in psychology. Today, as this text makes patently clear, ample work is available for the psychology graduate who wants to use his or her major in the areas of residential care, social and human services, human resources management, therapy, and teaching. And each of these areas has far more byways along the possible career path than any one book could outline.

Not many years ago, a support group for men dealing with prostate cancer and its effects would have been unfathomable. Now, men dealing with issues of impotence, incontinence, and loss of self-esteem and identity are able to come together with a facilitator and discuss, in a healing and supportive way, their challenges and successes in battling this disease. Many participants dramatically credit their lives to the support group. The leader of such a group may be an individual with a bachelor's or master's degree in psychology.

Psychologists now fill many roles—they are teachers, researchers, service providers (assessing needs, providing treatment), administrators (hospitals, government agencies, schools), and consultants (advising on problems in organizations, designing surveys, and organizing new patient systems).

Graduates today want to work with their psychology degree and find more opportunities to do so in drug intervention, institutions and halfway houses for individuals with mental illnesses and/or mental handicaps, testing, group-home counseling, geriatric counseling, youth center management, employment counseling, family planning, and biofeedback.

Psychology: A Future of Growth and Change

Any field growing as fast as psychology is going to give the appearance of disharmony or confusion as it speeds along its exponential growth curve toward some kind of maturity, if only in chronological terms. The membership of the American Psychological Association (APA) grows; the number of books and journals produced each year multiplies and so do the arguments, controversies, and legal and ethical issues that such growth naturally incurs. Specialization increases, and just as the APA counts more than fifty subspecialties among its membership, there are infinitely more areas of study in psychology, some of them extremely narrow. Within this text we discuss some of the current issues, including counselor/therapist relations, drug therapy, and the efficacy of various interventions that impact and influence career paths in psychology.

To suggest or attempt to outline the future of a field of study as diverse as psychology would be an imprudent exercise. Individuals called "psychologists" can be working on issues as diverse as sound perceptivity or the causes of depression. George Miller, quoted in Sigmund Koch and David E. Leary's *A Century of Psychology as Science*, has called psychology an "intellectual zoo." Psychology is really many psychologies, and as you read about the field and all these disparate sciences, you begin to get the merest hint of the struggle of the psychological community to find some unifying theme or umbrella philosophy to unite itself.

Just as the general public is confused about the work of psychologists, it is equally confused about who practices psychology. Many people believe that all psychology practitioners are doctors. While nearly all APA members do hold a doctorate, tens of thousands of individuals with bachelor's and master's degrees work in psychology. They perform testing, counseling, supervised therapy, and a variety of psychology-related tasks in schools, clinics, group homes, hospitals, and private practices.

Social problems in the latter half of the twentieth century multiplied, aggravated by economic and social influences. Homelessness, alienation, the breakdown of the nuclear family, the threat of violence, and social and racial tensions have only served to increase the need for those pursuing a career in psychology. As social symptoms multiply and the difficulties increase, the need for skilled help at all levels becomes apparent. The ability for even those with a bachelor's degree to make a contribution is evident.

A recent survey of articles in the national press reveals the following conditions impacting on the behavior and the mental health of individuals and groups:

- AD/HD
- Agoraphobia
- AIDS
- Alcoholism
- Alienation
- Alzheimer's disease
- Battering
- Depression
- Drug abuse
- Gang violence
- Job loss
- Light-affective syndrome
- Molestation

Today's graduates might have faced at least some of these problems in their own lives and, for many, this is part of their desire to use their psychology degree directly in their careers. Each area of concentration presages multiple possibilities for the career-minded psychology graduate.

Psychology is a science of great fertility, exploration, and dynamic change. Not only do we keep finding new areas of exploration, but new careers continue to appear as disciplines overlap and cross-disciplinary projects appear. The future of psychology might not be in "perspectives" and might not revolve around one particular area of concentration, but we do know that nothing need remain remote from psychological scrutiny.

PART ONE

THE JOB SEARCH

The Self-Assessment

Self-assessment is the process by which you begin to acknowledge your own particular blend of education, experiences, values, needs, and goals. It provides the foundation for career planning and the entire job search process. Self-assessment involves looking inward and asking yourself what can sometimes prove to be difficult questions. This self-examination should lead to an intimate understanding of your personal traits and values, consumption patterns and economic needs, longer-term goals, skill base, preferred skills, and underdeveloped skills.

You come to the self-assessment process knowing yourself well in some of these areas, but you may still be uncertain about other aspects. You may be well aware of your consumption patterns, but have you spent much time specifically identifying your longer-term goals or your personal values as they relate to work? No matter what level of self-assessment you have undertaken to date, it is now time to clarify all of these issues and questions as they relate to the job search.

The knowledge you gain in the self-assessment process will guide the rest of your job search. In this book, you will learn about all of the following tasks:

- Writing résumés and cover letters
- Researching careers and networking
- Interviewing and job offer considerations

In each of these steps, you will rely on and often return to the understanding gained through your self-assessment. Any individual seeking employment must be able and willing to express these facets of his or her personality to recruiters and interviewers throughout the job search. This communication allows you to show the world who you are so that together with employers you can determine whether there will be a workable match with a given job or career path.

How to Conduct a Self-Assessment

The self-assessment process goes on naturally all the time. People ask you to clarify what you mean, you make a purchasing decision, or you begin a new relationship. You react to the world and the world reacts to you. How you understand these interactions and any changes you might make because of them are part of the natural process of self-discovery. There is, however, a more comprehensive and efficient way to approach self-assessment with regard to employment.

Because self-assessment can become a complex exercise, we have distilled it into a seven-step process that provides an effective basis for undertaking a job search. The seven steps include the following:

1. Understanding your personal traits
2. Identifying your personal values
3. Calculating your economic needs
4. Exploring your longer-term goals
5. Enumerating your skill base
6. Recognizing your preferred skills
7. Assessing skills needing further development

As you work through your self-assessment, you might want to create a worksheet similar to the one shown in Exhibit 1.1, starting on the following page. Or you might want to keep a journal of the thoughts you have as you undergo this process. There will be many opportunities to revise your self-assessment as you start down the path of seeking a career.

Step 1 Understand Your Personal Traits
Each person has a unique personality that he or she brings to the job search process. Gaining a better understanding of your personal traits can help you evaluate job and career choices. Identifying these traits and then finding employment that allows you to draw on at least some of them can create a rewarding and fulfilling work experience. If potential employment doesn't allow you to use these preferred traits, it is important to decide whether you

Exhibit 1.1
SELF-ASSESSMENT WORKSHEET

Step 1. Understand Your Personal Traits

The personal traits that describe me are
(Include all of the words that describe you.)
The ten personal traits that most accurately describe me are
(List these ten traits.)

Step 2. Identify Your Personal Values

Working conditions that are important to me include
(List working conditions that would have to exist for you to accept a position.)
The values that go along with my working conditions are
(Write down the values that correspond to each working condition.)
Some additional values I've decided to include are
(List those values you identify as you conduct this job search.)

Step 3. Calculate Your Economic Needs

My estimated minimum annual salary requirement is
(Write the salary you have calculated based on your budget.)
Starting salaries for the positions I'm considering are
(List the name of each job you are considering and the associated starting salary.)

Step 4. Explore Your Longer-Term Goals

My thoughts on longer-term goals right now are
(Jot down some of your longer-term goals as you know them right now.)

Step 5. Enumerate Your Skill Base

The general skills I possess are
(List the skills that underlie tasks you are able to complete.)
The specific skills I possess are
(List more technical or specific skills that you possess, and indicate your level of expertise.)
General and specific skills that I want to promote to employers for the jobs I'm considering are
(List general and specific skills for each type of job you are considering.)

continued

Step 6. Recognize Your Preferred Skills

Skills that I would like to use on the job include

(List skills that you hope to use on the job, and indicate how often you'd like to use them.)

Step 7. Assess Skills Needing Further Development

Some skills that I'll need to acquire for the jobs I'm considering include

(Write down skills listed in job advertisements or job descriptions that you don't currently possess.)

I believe I can build these skills by

(Describe how you plan to acquire these skills.)

---

can find other ways to express them or whether you would be better off not considering this type of job. Interests and hobbies pursued outside of work hours can be one way to use personal traits you don't have an opportunity to draw on in your work. For example, if you consider yourself an outgoing person and the kinds of jobs you are examining allow little contact with other people, you may be able to achieve the level of interaction that is comfortable for you outside of your work setting. If such a compromise seems impractical or otherwise unsatisfactory, you probably should explore only jobs that provide the interaction you want and need on the job.

Many young adults who are not very confident about their employability will downplay their need for income. They will say, "Money is not all that important if I love my work." But if you begin to document exactly what you need for housing, transportation, insurance, clothing, food, and utilities, you will begin to understand that some jobs cannot meet your financial needs and it doesn't matter how wonderful the job is. If you have to worry each payday about bills and other financial obligations, you won't be very effective on the job. Begin now to be honest with yourself about your needs.

Begin the self-assessment process by creating an inventory of your personal traits. Make a list of as many words as possible to describe yourself. Words like *accurate, creative, future-oriented, relaxed,* or *structured* are just a few examples. In addition, you might ask people who know you well how they might describe you.

Focus on Selected Personal Traits. Of all the traits you identified, select the ten you believe most accurately describe you. Keep track of these ten traits.

Consider Your Personal Traits in the Job Search Process. As you begin exploring jobs and careers, watch for matches between your personal traits and the job descriptions you read. Some jobs will require many personal traits you know you possess, and others will not seem to match those traits.

A youth counselor's work at a secure, clinically intensive residential treatment program serving emotionally disturbed adolescents ages twelve to eighteen requires self-control, confidence, and trustworthiness. Counselors in this type of facility are pivotal members of treatment teams. Exceptional communications skills are required for the crisis management and de-escalation techniques required in group counseling sessions. These same skills are used by the youth counselor in helping the clients learn social skills, enhance family connections, and survive peer pressure.

Your ability to respond to changing conditions, your decision-making ability, productivity, creativity, and verbal skills all have a bearing on your success in and enjoyment of your work life. To better guarantee success, be sure to take the time needed to understand these traits in yourself.

Step 2 Identify Your Personal Values

Your personal values affect every aspect of your life, including employment, and they develop and change as you move through life. Values can be defined as principles that we hold in high regard, qualities that are important and desirable to us. Some values aren't ordinarily connected to work (love, beauty, color, light, relationships, family, or religion), and others are (autonomy, cooperation, effectiveness, achievement, knowledge, and security). Our values determine, in part, the level of satisfaction we feel in a particular job.

Define Acceptable Working Conditions. One facet of employment is the set of working conditions that must exist for someone to consider taking a job.

Each of us would probably create a unique list of acceptable working conditions, but items that might be included on many people's lists are the amount of money you would need to be paid, how far you are willing to drive or travel, the amount of freedom you want in determining your own schedule, whether you would be working with people or data or things, and the types of tasks you would be willing to do. Your conditions might include statements of working conditions you will *not* accept; for example, you might not be willing to work at night or on weekends or holidays.

If you were offered a job tomorrow, what conditions would have to exist for you to realistically consider accepting the position? Take some time and make a list of these conditions.

Realize Associated Values. Your list of working conditions can be used to create an inventory of your values relating to jobs and careers you are exploring. For example, if one of your conditions stated that you wanted to earn at least $30,000 per year, the associated value would be financial gain. If another condition was that you wanted to work with a friendly group of people, the value that went along with that might be belonging or interaction with people.

Relate Your Values to the World of Work. As you read the job descriptions you come across either in this book, in newspapers and magazines, or online, think about the values associated with each position.

The duties of a human resources assistant would include planning co-op and intern events; organizing, coordinating, and designing event communications for managers and co-op students; and assisting with new-hire paperwork. Associated values are organization, communication, creativity, and interaction.

At least some of the associated values in the field you're exploring should match those you extracted from your list of working conditions. Take a second look at any values that don't match up. How important are they to you? What will happen if they are not satisfied on the job? Can you incorporate those personal values elsewhere? Your answers need to be brutally honest. As you continue your exploration, be sure to add to your list any additional values that occur to you.

Step 3 Calculate Your Economic Needs
Each of us grew up in an environment that provided for certain basic needs, such as food and shelter, and, to varying degrees, other needs that we now consider basic, such as cable television, e-mail, or an automobile. Needs such as privacy, space, and quiet, which at first glance may not appear to be mon-

etary needs, may add to housing expenses and so should be considered as you examine your economic needs. For example, if you place a high value on a large, open living space for yourself, it would be difficult to satisfy that need without an associated high housing cost, especially in a densely populated city environment.

As you prepare to move into the world of work and become responsible for meeting your own basic needs, it is important to consider the salary you will need to be able to afford a satisfying standard of living. The three-step process outlined here will help you plan a budget, which in turn will allow you to evaluate the various career choices and geographic locations you are considering. The steps include (1) develop a realistic budget, (2) examine starting salaries, and (3) use a cost-of-living index.

Develop a Realistic Budget. Each of us has certain expectations for the kind of lifestyle we want to maintain. To begin the process of defining your economic needs, it will be helpful to determine what you expect to spend on routine monthly expenses. These expenses include housing, food, transportation, entertainment, utilities, loan repayments, and revolving charge accounts. You may not currently spend anything for certain items, but you probably will have to once you begin supporting yourself. As you develop this budget, be generous in your estimates, but keep in mind any items that could be reduced or eliminated. If you are not sure about the cost of a certain item, talk with family or friends who would be able to give you a realistic estimate.

If this is new or difficult for you, start to keep a log of expenses right now. You may be surprised at how much you actually spend each month for food or stamps or magazines. Household expenses and personal grooming items can often loom very large in a budget, as can auto repairs or home maintenance.

Income taxes must also be taken into consideration when examining salary requirements. State and local taxes vary, so it is difficult to calculate exactly the effect of taxes on the amount of income you need to generate. To roughly estimate the gross income necessary to generate your minimum annual salary requirement, multiply the minimum salary you have calculated by a factor of 1.35. The resulting figure will be an approximation of what your gross income would need to be, given your estimated expenses.

Examine Starting Salaries. Starting salaries for each of the career tracks are provided throughout this book. These salary figures can be used in conjunction with the cost-of-living index (discussed in the next section) to determine whether you would be able to meet your basic economic needs in a given geographic location.

Use a Cost-of-Living Index. If you are thinking about trying to get a job in a geographic region other than the one where you now live, understanding differences in the cost of living will help you come to a more informed decision about making a move. By using a cost-of-living index, you can compare salaries offered and the cost of living in different locations with what you know about the salaries offered and the cost of living in your present location.

Many variables are used to calculate the cost-of-living index. Often included are housing, groceries, utilities, transportation, health care, clothing, and entertainment expenses. Right now you do not need to worry about the details associated with calculating a given index. The main purpose of this exercise is to help you understand that pay ranges for entry-level positions may not vary greatly, but the cost of living in different locations *can* vary tremendously.

Let's say you want to find a job in human resources as a training specialist in a large metropolitan community and you currently live in Oklahoma City, Oklahoma. According to information contained on the American Society for Training & Development website (http://astd.salary.com), a training specialist's salary varies according to geographic location. As of the date this book was published, the estimated average beginning training specialist salaries in three cities were $38,665 in Atlanta, Georgia; $36,434 in Oklahoma City, Oklahoma; and $36,165 in Grand Forks, North Dakota.

Although the average beginning salary is highest in Atlanta and lowest in Grand Forks, if you will be relocating to either of those cities you need to take into account the cost of living in each place to fully understand the impact of the salary you would earn there. For example, a comparison of the living expenses in Oklahoma City and Atlanta indicates that you would need to make $42,620 in Atlanta to maintain the same purchasing power as you would have with a $36,434 salary in Oklahoma City. Even an annual salary that is 6.1 percent higher ($38,665) in Atlanta is not enough to compensate for the 17 percent increase in the cost of living there. So, if you moved to Atlanta from Oklahoma City, you would experience a loss of almost $4,000 in disposable income.

> Groceries are 10 percent higher in Atlanta.
> Housing is 6 percent higher.
> Utilities are 8 percent higher.
> Transportation is 3 percent higher.
> Health care is 8 percent higher
> Miscellaneous goods/services are 5 percent higher.

If a change in a training specialist position involves moving from Oklahoma City to Grand Forks, North Dakota, you would need to earn $39,416 in Grand Forks to have the same purchasing power as In Oklahoma City—the cost of living in Grand Forks is 8.2 percent higher than in Oklahoma City. Remember, the average beginning training specialist salary in Grand Forks is $36,165, so the lower salary would mean a loss of almost $3,300 in disposable income. Cost comparisons show:

> Groceries are 14 percent higher in Grand Forks.
> Housing is 4 percent higher.
> Utilities are 12 percent higher.
> Transportation is 10 percent lower.
> Health care is 3 percent lower.
> Miscellaneous goods/services are 3 percent lower.

You also need to evaluate whether an opportunity for employment that involves relocating to a different geographic location will advance your career or meet personal needs. Other cities may have more opportunities for advancement, but you need to make sure that relocating will be financially feasible.

You can work through a similar exercise for any type of job you are considering and for many locations when current salary information is available. It will be worth your time to undertake this analysis if you are seriously considering a relocation. By doing so you will be able to make an informed choice.

Step 4   Explore Your Longer-Term Goals

There is no question that when we first begin working, our goals are to use our skills and education in a job that will reward us with employment, income, and status relative to the preparation we brought with us to this position. If we are not being paid as much as we feel we should for our level of education or if job demands don't provide the intellectual stimulation we had hoped for, we experience unhappiness and as a result often seek other employment.

Most jobs we consider "good" are those that fulfill our basic "lower-level" needs of security, food, clothing, shelter, income, and productive work. But even when our basic needs are met and our jobs are secure and productive, we as individuals are constantly changing. As we change, the demands and expectations we place on our jobs may change. Fortunately, some jobs grow and change with us, and this explains why some people are happy throughout many years in a job.

But more often people are bigger than the jobs they fill. We have more goals and needs than any job could satisfy. These are "higher-level" needs of self-esteem, companionship, affection, and an increasing desire to feel we are employing ourselves in the most effective way possible. Not all of these higher-level needs can be met through employment, but for as long as we are employed, we increasingly demand that our jobs play their part in moving us along the path to fulfillment.

Another obvious but important fact is that we change as we mature. Although our jobs also have the potential for change, they may not change as frequently or as markedly as we do. There are increasingly fewer one-job, one-employer careers; we must think about a work future that may involve voluntary or forced moves from employer to employer. Because of that very real possibility, we need to take advantage of the opportunities in each position we hold. Acquiring the skills and competencies associated with each position will keep us viable and attractive as employees. This is particularly true in a job market that not only is technology/computer dependent, but also is populated with more and more small, self-transforming organizations rather than the large, seemingly stable organizations of the past.

If you are considering a career in social rehabilitation counseling, you would gain a solid understanding of this path if you talked to an entry-level counselor, a more experienced and senior counselor, and, finally, someone who has risen through the ranks and who is now serving as the head of the department. Each will have his or her own unique perspective and concerns as well as different value priorities.

Step 5 Enumerate Your Skill Base

In terms of the job search, skills can be thought of as capabilities that can be developed in school, at work, or by volunteering and then used in specific job settings. Many studies have documented the kinds of skills that employers seek in entry-level applicants. For example, some of the most desired skills for individuals interested in the teaching profession are the ability to interact effectively with students one-on-one, to manage a classroom, to adapt to varying situations as necessary, and to get involved in school activities. Business employers have also identified important qualities, including enthusiasm for the employer's product or service, a businesslike mind, the ability to follow written or oral instructions, the ability to demonstrate self control, the confidence to suggest new ideas, the ability to communicate with all members of a group, an awareness of cultural differences, and loyalty, to name just a few. You will find that many of these skills are also in the repertoire of qualities demanded in your college major.

To be successful in obtaining any given job, you must be able to demonstrate that you possess a certain mix of skills that will allow you to carry out the duties required by that job. This skill mix will vary a great deal from job to job; to determine the skills necessary for the jobs you are seeking, you can read job advertisements or more generic job descriptions, such as those found later in this book. If you want to be effective in the job search, you must directly show employers that you possess the skills needed to be successful in filling the position. These skills will initially be described on your résumé and then discussed again during the interview process.

Skills are either general or specific. To develop a list of skills relevant to employers, you must first identify the general skills you possess, then list specific skills you have to offer, and, finally, examine which of these skills employers are seeking.

Identify Your General Skills. Because you possess or will possess a college degree, employers will assume that you can read and write, perform certain basic computations, think critically, and communicate effectively. Employers will want to see that you have acquired these skills, and they will want to know which additional general skills you possess.

One way to begin identifying skills is to write an experiential diary. An experiential diary lists all the tasks you were responsible for completing for each job you've held and then outlines the skills required to do those tasks. You may list several skills for any given task. This diary allows you to distinguish between the tasks you performed and the underlying skills required to complete those tasks. Here's an example:

Tasks	Skills
Answering telephone	Effective use of language, clear diction, ability to direct inquiries, ability to solve problems
Waiting on tables	Poise under conditions of time and pressure, speed, accuracy, good memory, simultaneous completion of tasks, sales skills

For each job or experience you have participated in, develop a worksheet based on the example shown here. On a résumé, you may want to describe these skills rather than simply listing tasks. Skills are easier for the employer to appreciate, especially when your experience is very different from the employment you are seeking. In addition to helping you identify general skills, this experiential diary will prepare you to speak more effectively in an interview about the qualifications you possess.

Identify Your Specific Skills. It may be easier to identify your specific skills because you can definitely say whether you can speak other languages, program a computer, draft a map or diagram, or edit a document using appropriate symbols and terminology.

Using your experiential diary, identify the points in your history where you learned how to do something very specific, and decide whether you have a beginning, intermediate, or advanced knowledge of how to use that particular skill. Right now, be sure to list *every* specific skill you have, and don't consider whether you like using the skill. Write down a list of specific skills you have acquired and the level of competence you possess—beginning, intermediate, or advanced.

Relate Your Skills to Employers. You probably have thought about a couple of different jobs you might be interested in obtaining, and one way to begin relating the general and specific skills you possess to a potential employer's needs is to read actual advertisements for these types of positions (see Part Two for resources listing actual job openings).

For example, you might be interested in working as a family counselor. A typical job listing might read, "Provide counseling and case management services to children and families in their own homes. Focus on family but also address school, peers, community, and other systems that affect the child and family. Requires bachelor's with one to two years' experience working with emotionally disturbed children." If you then use any one of a number of general sources of information that describe the job of family counselor, you would find additional information. Family counselors also complete required paperwork, help design innovative service programs, and refer family members to psychiatric resources as needed.

Begin building a comprehensive list of required skills with the first job description you read. Exploring online job advertisements of several related positions will reveal important core skills that are necessary for obtaining the type of work you're interested in. In building this list, include both general and specific skills.

The following is a sample list of skills needed to be successful as a family counselor. These items were extracted from both general resources and actual job listings.

JOB: FAMILY COUNSELOR

General Skills	Specific Skills
Commit to positive outcomes	Resolve emotional conflicts between parents and children
Exhibit high level of energy	
Manage day-to-day scheduling	
Participate actively as part of a team	Modify parents' behavior toward their children
Gather information	Modify children's behavior toward their parents
	Implement Multisystemic Therapy Model
	Manage caseload of five families with three-month treatment length

Try to generate a comprehensive list of required skills for at least one job you are considering.

The list of general skills that you develop for a given career path will be valuable for any number of jobs you might apply for. Many of the specific skills would also be transferable to other types of positions. For example, providing skills coaching is a required skill for some family counselors, and it would be required of some social rehabilitation counselors as well.

Step 6 Recognize Your Preferred Skills

In the previous section you developed a comprehensive list of skills that relate to particular career paths that are of interest to you. You can now relate these to skills that you prefer to use. We all use a wide range of skills (some researchers say individuals have a repertoire of about five hundred skills), but we may not particularly be interested in using all of them in our work. There may be some skills that come to us more naturally or that we use successfully time and time again and that we want to continue to use; these are best described as our preferred skills. For this exercise use the list of skills that you created for the previous section, and decide which of them you are *most interested in using* in future work and how often you would like to use them. You might be interested in using some skills only occasionally, while others you would like to use more regularly. You probably also have skills that you hope you can use constantly.

As you examine job announcements, look for matches between this list of preferred skills and the qualifications described in the advertisements. These skills should be highlighted on your résumé and discussed in job interviews.

Step 7 Assess Skills Needing Further Development

Previously you compiled a list of general and specific skills required for given positions. You already possess some of these skills; those that remain to be developed are your underdeveloped skills.

If you are just beginning the job search, there may be gaps between the qualifications required for some of the jobs you're considering and the skills you possess. The thought of having to admit to and talk about these underdeveloped skills, especially in a job interview, is a frightening one. One way to put a healthy perspective on this subject is to target and relate your exploration of underdeveloped skills to the types of positions you are seeking. Recognizing these shortcomings and planning to overcome them with either on-the-job training or additional formal education can be a positive way to address the concept of underdeveloped skills.

On your worksheet or in your journal, make a list of up to five general or specific skills required for the positions you're interested in that you *don't currently possess*. For each item list an idea you have for specific action you could take to acquire that skill. Do some brainstorming to come up with possible actions. If you have a hard time generating ideas, talk to people currently working in this type of position, professionals in your college career services office, trusted friends, family members, or members of related professional associations.

In the chapter on interviewing, we will discuss in detail how to effectively address questions about underdeveloped skills. Generally speaking, though, employers want genuine answers to these types of questions. They want you to reveal "the real you," and they also want to see how you answer difficult questions. In taking the positive, targeted approach discussed previously, you show the employer that you are willing to continue to learn and that you have a plan for strengthening your job qualifications.

Use Your Self-Assessment

Exploring entry-level career options can be an exciting experience if you have good resources available and will take the time to use them. Can you effectively complete the following tasks?

1. Understand your personality traits and relate them to career choices
2. Define your personal values
3. Determine your economic needs
4. Explore longer-term goals
5. Understand your skill base
6. Recognize your preferred skills
7. Express a willingness to improve on your underdeveloped skills

If so, then you can more meaningfully participate in the job search process by writing a more effective résumé, finding job titles that represent work you are interested in doing, locating job sites that will provide the opportunity for you to use your strengths and skills, networking in an informed way, participating in focused interviews, getting the most out of follow-up contacts, and evaluating job offers to find those that create a good match between you and the employer. The remaining chapters in Part One guide you through these next steps in the job search process. For many job seekers, this process can take anywhere from three months to a year to implement. The time you will need to put into your job search will depend on the type of job you want and the geographic location where you'd like to work. Think of your effort as a job in itself, requiring you to set aside time each week to complete the needed work. Carefully undertaken efforts may reduce the time you need for your job search.

2

The Résumé and Cover Letter

The task of writing a résumé may seem overwhelming if you are unfamiliar with this type of document, but there are some easily understood techniques that can and should be used. This section was written to help you understand the purpose of the résumé, the different types of formats available, and how to write the sections that contain information traditionally found on a résumé. We will present examples and explanations that address questions frequently posed by people writing their first résumé or updating an old one.

Even within the formats and suggestions given, however, there are infinite variations. True, most follow one of the outlines suggested, but you should feel free to adjust the résumé to suit your needs and make it expressive of your life and experience.

Why Write a Résumé?

The purpose of a résumé is to convince an employer that you should be interviewed. Whether you're mailing, faxing, or e-mailing this document, you'll want to present enough information to show that you can make an immediate and valuable contribution to an organization. A résumé is not an indepth historical or legal document; later in the job search process you may be asked to document your entire work history on an application form and attest to its validity. The résumé should, instead, highlight relevant information pertaining directly to the organization that will receive the document or to the type of position you are seeking.

We will discuss the chronological and digital résumés in detail here. Functional and targeted résumés, which are used much less often, are briefly discussed. The reasons for using one type of résumé over another and the typical format for each are addressed in the following sections.

The Chronological Résumé

The chronological résumé is the most common of the various résumé formats and therefore the format that employers are most used to receiving. This type of résumé is easy to read and understand because it details the chronological progression of jobs you have held. (See Exhibit 2.1.) It begins with your most recent employment and works back in time. If you have a solid work history or have experience that provided growth and development in your duties and responsibilities, a chronological résumé will highlight these achievements. The typical elements of a chronological résumé include the heading, a career objective, educational background, employment experience, activities, and references.

The Heading
The heading consists of your name, address, telephone number, and other means of contact. This may include a fax number, e-mail address, and your home-page address. If you are using a shared e-mail account or a parent's business fax, be sure to let others who use these systems know that you may receive important professional correspondence via these systems. You wouldn't want to miss a vital e-mail or fax! Likewise, if your résumé directs readers to a personal home page on the Web, be certain it's a professional personal home page designed to be viewed and appreciated by a prospective employer. This may mean making substantial changes in the home page you currently mount on the Web.

The Objective
Without a doubt the objective statement is the most challenging part of the résumé for most writers. Even for individuals who have decided on a career path, it can be difficult to encapsulate all they want to say in one or two brief sentences. For job seekers who are unfocused or unclear about their intentions, trying to write this section can inhibit the entire résumé writing process.

Keep the objective as short as possible and no longer than two short sentences.

Exhibit 2.1
CHRONOLOGICAL RÉSUMÉ

OLIVIA HAYFARMER

<u>School Address</u>
Student Apartments #25
Oakland University
Rochester, MI 48309
(248) 555-1212
ohayfarm@xxx.net
(until May 2007)

<u>Permanent Address</u>
555 S. Main St.
Rochester Hills, MI 48307
(248) 555-1212
ohayfarm@xxx.net

OBJECTIVE
Entry-level position in an independent living residential home. Special interest in clientele facing drug and alcohol dependency.

EDUCATION
Bachelor of Arts in Psychology
Oakland University, Rochester, MI

EXPERIENCE
Intern, Sobriety Home, Inc., Detroit, MI, Jan. 2007–Present.
Work as a therapist's assistant at a substance abuse halfway house. Use a variety of software packages to maintain various types of records, including insurance records; transcribe therapist's notes; and respond to questions from insurers.

Women's Shelter Volunteer, Detroit, MI, Sept. 2005–Jan. 2007.
Worked as awake overnight residential counselor twice a month. Admitted new residents, assigned residents an area to sleep, worked with team of counselors to follow up on each admission. Assisted new residents in obtaining available services.

Admissions Tour Guide, Oakland University, Rochester, MI, Sept. 2005–Dec. 2006.
Led campus tours for prospective students and parents, responding to a wide variety of questions. Called prospective students, and assisted with various office duties.

continued

Reporter, The Oakland Post student newspaper, Oakland University, Jan. 2004–
Dec. 2004.
On a weekly basis, attended special events on campus (lectures, cultural events,
etc.) and wrote associated stories.

ACTIVITIES
Spanish Club, active member, three years. Women's Center volunteer, two
years, Intramural softball, one year.

REFERENCES
Excellent professional references available upon request.

Choose one of the following types of objective statement:

1. General Objective Statement

- An entry-level educational programming coordinator position

2. Position-Focused Objective

- To obtain the position of conference coordinator at State College

3. Industry-Focused Objective

- To begin a career as a sales representative in the cruise line industry

4. Summary of Qualifications Statement

A degree in psychology and three years of growing job responsibility in a women's shelter have prepared me to begin a career
as an independent living counselor with a social service agency
that values a thoughtful team player and detailed case-file note
taker.

Support Your Objective. A résumé that contains any one of these types
of objective statements should then go on to demonstrate why you are qual-

ified to get the position. Listing academic degrees can be one way to indicate qualifications. Another demonstration would be in the way previous experiences, both volunteer and paid, are described. Without this kind of documentation in the body of the résumé, the objective looks unsupported. Think of the résumé as telling a connected story about you. All the elements should work together to form a coherent picture that ideally should relate to your statement of objective.

Education

This section of your résumé should indicate the exact name of the degree you will receive or have received, spelled out completely with no abbreviations. The degree is generally listed after the objective, followed by the institution name and location, and then the month and year of graduation. This section could also include your academic minor, grade point average (GPA), and appearance on the Dean's List or President's List.

If you have enough space, you might want to include a section listing courses related to the field in which you are seeking work. The best use of a "related courses" section would be to list some course work that is not traditionally associated with the major. Perhaps you took several computer courses outside your degree that will be helpful and related to the job prospects you are entertaining. Several education section examples are shown here:

- Bachelor of Arts in Interdisciplinary Studies, a self-designed program concentrating on interpersonal relations and business; Bristol University; Bristol, TN; May 2007
- Bachelor of Science Degree in Psychology; University of North Dakota; Grand Forks, ND; December 2007; minor: Communications
- Bachelor of Science Degree in Psychology; Columbia College; Columbia, IL; May 2007

An example of a format for a related courses section follows:

RELATED COURSES	
Desktop Publishing	Computer Graphics
Group Counseling	Human Resources Management
Technical Writing	Organizational Communications

Experience

The experience section of your résumé should be the most substantial part and should take up most of the space on the page. Employers want to see what kind of work history you have. They will look at your range of experiences, longevity in jobs, and specific tasks you are able to complete. This section may also be called "work experience," "related experience," "employment history," or "employment." No matter what you call this section, some important points to remember are the following:

1. **Describe your duties** as they relate to the position you are seeking.
2. **Emphasize major responsibilities** and indicate increases in responsibility. Include all relevant employment experiences: summer, part-time, internships, cooperative education, or self-employment.
3. **Emphasize skills**, especially those that transfer from one situation to another. The fact that you coordinated a student organization, chaired meetings, supervised others, and managed a budget leads one to suspect that you could coordinate other things as well.
4. **Use descriptive job titles** that provide information about what you did. A "Student Intern" should be more specifically stated as, for example, "Magazine Operations Intern." "Volunteer" is also too general; a title such as "Peer Writing Tutor" would be more appropriate.
5. **Create word pictures** by using active verbs to start sentences. Describe *results* you have produced in the work you have done.

A limp description would say something such as the following: "My duties included helping with production, proofreading, and editing. I used a design and page layout program." An action statement would be stated as follows: "Coordinated and assisted in the creative marketing of brochures and seminar promotions, becoming proficient in Quark."

Remember, an accomplishment is simply a result, a final measurable product that people can relate to. A duty is not a result; it is an obligation—every job holder has duties. For an effective résumé, list as many results as you can. To make the most of the limited space you have and to give your description impact, carefully select appropriate and accurate descriptors.

Here are some traits that employers tell us they like to see:

- Teamwork
- Energy and motivation

- Learning and using new skills
- Versatility
- Critical thinking
- Understanding how profits are created
- Organizational acumen
- Communicating directly and clearly, in both writing and speaking
- Risk taking
- Willingness to admit mistakes
- High personal standards

Solutions to Frequently Encountered Problems

Repetitive Employment with the Same Employer

EMPLOYMENT: The Foot Locker, Portland, Oregon. Summer 2001, 2002, 2003. Initially employed in high school as salesclerk. Because of successful performance, asked to return next two summers at higher pay with added responsibility. Ranked as the #2 salesperson the first summer and #1 the next two summers. Assisted in arranging eye-catching retail displays; served as manager of other summer workers during owner's absence.

A Large Number of Jobs

EMPLOYMENT: Recent Hospitality Industry Experience: Affiliated with four upscale hotel/restaurant complexes (September 2001–February 2004), where I worked part- and full-time as a waiter, bartender, disc jockey, and bookkeeper to produce income for college.

Several Positions with the Same Employer

EMPLOYMENT: Coca-Cola Bottling Co., Burlington, Vermont, 2001–2004. In four years, I received three promotions, each with increased pay and responsibility.

Summer Sales Coordinator: Promoted to hire, train, and direct efforts of add-on staff of fifteen college-age route salespeople hired to meet summer peak demand for product.

Sales Administrator: Promoted to run home office sales desk, managing accounts and associated delivery schedules for professional sales force of ten people. Intensive phone work, daily interaction with all personnel, and strong knowledge of product line required.

Route Salesperson: Summer employment to travel and tourism industry sites that use Coke products. Met specific schedule demands, used good communication skills with wide variety of customers, and demonstrated strong selling skills. Named salesperson of the month for July and August of that year.

Questions Résumé Writers Often Ask

How Far Back Should I Go in Terms of Listing Past Jobs?
Usually, listing three or four jobs should suffice. If you did something back in high school that has a bearing on your future aspirations for employment, by all means list the job. As you progress through your college career, high school jobs will be replaced on the résumé by college employment.

Should I Differentiate Between Paid and Nonpaid Employment?
Most employers are not initially concerned about how much you were paid. They are eager to know how much responsibility you held in your past employment. There is no need to specify that your work was as a volunteer if you had significant responsibilities.

How Should I Represent My Accomplishments or Work-Related Responsibilities?
Succinctly, but fully. In other words, give the employer enough information to arouse curiosity but not so much detail that you leave nothing to the imagination. Besides, some jobs merit more lengthy explanations than others. Be sure to convey any information that can give an employer a better understanding of the depth of your involvement at work. Did you supervise others? How many? Did your efforts result in a more efficient operation? How much did you increase efficiency? Did you handle a budget? How much? Were you promoted in a short time? Did you work two jobs at once or fifteen hours per week after high school? Where appropriate, quantify.

Should the Work Section Always Follow the Education Section on the Résumé?
Always lead with your strengths. If your education closely relates to the employment you now seek, put this section after the objective. If your edu-

cation does not closely relate but you have a surplus of good work experiences, consider reversing the order of your sections to lead with employment, followed by education.

How Should I Present My Activities, Honors, Awards, Professional Societies, and Affiliations?

This section of the résumé can add valuable information for an employer to consider if used correctly. The rule of thumb for information in this section is to include only those activities that are in some way relevant to the objective stated on your résumé. If you can draw a valid connection between your activities and your objective, include them; if not, leave them out.

Professional affiliations and honors should all be listed; especially important are those related to your job objective. Social clubs and activities need not be a part of your résumé unless you hold a significant office or you are looking for a position related to your membership. Be aware that most prospective employers' principal concerns are related to your employability, not your social life. If you have any, publications can be included as an addendum to your résumé.

How Should I Handle References?

The use of references is considered a part of the interview process, and they should never be listed on a résumé. You would always provide references to a potential employer if requested to, so it is not even necessary to include this section on the résumé if space does not permit. If space is available, it is acceptable to include the following statement:

- References furnished upon request.

The Functional Résumé

A functional résumé departs from a chronological résumé in that it organizes information by specific accomplishments in various settings: previous jobs, volunteer work, associations, and so forth. This type of résumé permits you to stress the substance of your experiences rather than the position titles you have held. You should consider using a functional résumé if you have held a series of similar jobs that relied on the same skills or abilities. There are many good books in which you can find examples of functional résumés, including *How to Write a Winning Resume* or *Resumes Made Easy*.

The Targeted Résumé

The targeted résumé focuses on specific work-related capabilities you can bring to a given position within an organization. Past achievements are listed to highlight your capabilities and the work history section is abbreviated.

Digital Résumés

Today's employers have to manage an enormous number of résumés. One of the most frequent complaints the writers of this series hear from students is the failure of employers to even acknowledge the receipt of a résumé and cover letter. Frequently, the reason for this poor response or nonresponse is the volume of applications received for every job. In an attempt to better manage the considerable labor investment involved in processing large numbers of résumés, many employers are requiring digital submission of résumés. There are two types of digital résumés: those that can be e-mailed or posted to a website, called *electronic résumés*, and those that can be "read" by a computer, commonly called *scannable résumés*. Though the format may be a bit different from the traditional "paper" résumé, the goal of both types of digital résumés is the same—to get you an interview! These résumés must be designed to be "technologically friendly." What that basically means to you is that they should be free of graphics and fancy formatting. (See Exhibit 2.2.)

Electronic Résumés

Sometimes referred to as plain-text résumés, electronic résumés are designed to be e-mailed to an employer or posted to one of many commercial Internet databases such as Careerbuilder.com, America's Job Bank (ajb.dni.us), or Monster.com.

Some technical considerations:

- Electronic résumés must be written in American Standard Code for Information Interchange (ASCII), which is simply a plain-text format. These characters are universally recognized so that every computer can accurately read and understand them. To create an ASCII file of your current résumé, open your document, then save it as a text or ASCII file. This will eliminate all formatting. Edit as needed using your computer's text editor application.
- Use a standard-width typeface. Courier is a good choice because it is the font associated with ASCII in most systems.

Exhibit 2.2
DIGITAL RÉSUMÉ

OLIVIA HAYFARMER ◄─────────────────── Put your name at the
Student Apartments #25   top on its own line.
Oakland University
Rochester, MI 48309
(248) 555-1212 ◄─────────────────── Put your phone number
ohayfarm@xxx.net   on its own line.

KEYWORD SUMMARY ◄─────────
Counselor   Keywords make your
Independent living   résumé easier to find in
Drug dependency   a database.
Alcohol dependency

OBJECTIVE
Entry-level position in an independent living
residential home. Special interest in clientele   Use a standard-width
facing drug and alcohol dependency.   typeface.

EDUCATION
Bachelor of Arts in Psychology
Oakland University, Rochester, MI

EXPERIENCE
Intern, Sobriety Home, Inc., substance abuse
halfway house   Use a space between
* Work as therapist's assistant.   asterisk and text.
* Use variety of software packages to maintain
various records.
* Transcribe therapist's notes.   No line should exceed
* Respond to questions from insurers.   sixty-five characters.

Women's Shelter Volunteer, Oakland University,
Detroit, MI, Sept 2005-Jan. 2007.
* Worked as awake overnight residential counselor.
* Admitted new residents.

continued

* Assigned residents a place to sleep.
* Worked with counseling team to follow up on
each admission.
* Assisted new residents in obtaining available services.

ACTIVITIES ◄————————————————— Capitalize letters to
emphasize headings.

* Spanish Club, three years
* Women's Center volunteer, two years
* Intramural softball, one year

End each line by
hitting the ENTER key.

REFERENCES
Excellent professional references available upon request.

- Use a font size of 11 to 14 points. A 12-point font is considered standard.
- Your margin should be left-justified.
- Do not exceed sixty-five characters per line because the word-wrap function doesn't operate in ASCII.
- Do not use boldface, italics, underlining, bullets, or various font sizes. Instead, use asterisks, plus signs, or all capital letters when you want to emphasize something.
- Avoid graphics and shading.
- Use as many "keywords" as you possibly can. These are words or phrases usually relating to skills or experience that either are specifically used in the job announcement or are popular buzzwords in the industry.
- Minimize abbreviations.
- Your name should be the first line of text.
- Conduct a "test run" by e-mailing your résumé to yourself and a friend before you send it to the employer. See how it transmits, and make any changes you need to. Continue to test it until it's exactly how you want it to look.
- Unless an employer specifically requests that you send the résumé in the form of an attachment, don't. Employers can encounter problems opening a document as an attachment, and there are always viruses to consider.
- Don't forget your cover letter. Send it along with your résumé as a single message.

Scannable Résumés

Some companies are relying on technology to narrow the candidate pool for available job openings. Electronic Applicant Tracking uses imaging to scan, sort, and store résumé elements in a database. Then, through OCR (Optical Character Recognition) software, the computer scans the résumés for keywords and phrases. To have the best chance at getting an interview, you want to increase the number of "hits"—matches of your skills, abilities, experience, and education to those the computer is scanning for—your résumé will get. You can see how critical using the right keywords is for this type of résumé.

Technical considerations include:

- Again, do not use boldface (newer systems may be able to read this, but many older ones won't), italics, underlining, bullets, shading, graphics, or multiple font sizes. Instead, for emphasis, use asterisks, plus signs, or all capital letters. Minimize abbreviations.
- Use a popular typeface such as Courier, Helvetica, Arial, or Palatino. Avoid decorative fonts.
- Font size should be between 11 and 14 points.
- Do not compress the spacing between letters.
- Use horizontal and vertical lines sparingly; the computer may misread them as the letters L or I.
- Left-justify the text.
- Do not use parentheses or brackets around telephone numbers, and be sure your phone number is on its own line of text.
- Your name should be the first line of text and on its own line. If your résumé is longer than one page, be sure to put your name on the top of all pages.
- Use a traditional résumé structure. The chronological format may work best.
- Use nouns that are skill-focused, such as *management, writer,* and *programming.* This is different from traditional paper résumés, which use action-oriented verbs.
- Laser printers produce the finest copies. Avoid dot-matrix printers.
- Use standard, light-colored paper with text on one side only. Since the higher the contrast, the better, your best choice is black ink on white paper.
- Always send original copies. If you must fax, set the fax on fine mode, not standard.
- Do not staple or fold your résumé. This can confuse the computer.

- Before you send your scannable résumé, be certain the employer uses this technology. If you can't determine this, you may want to send two versions (scannable and traditional) to be sure your résumé gets considered.

Résumé Production and Other Tips

An ink-jet printer is the preferred option for printing your résumé. Begin by printing just a few copies. You may find a small error or you may simply want to make some changes, and it is less frustrating and less expensive if you print in small batches.

Résumé paper color should be carefully chosen. You should consider the types of employers who will receive your résumé and the types of positions for which you are applying. Use white or ivory paper for traditional or conservative employers or for higher-level positions.

Black ink on sharp, white paper can be harsh on the reader's eyes. Think about an ivory or cream paper that will provide less contrast and be easier to read. Pink, green, and blue tints should generally be avoided.

Many résumé writers buy packages of matching envelopes and cover sheet stationery that, although not absolutely necessary, help convey a professional impression.

If you'll be producing many cover letters at home, be sure you have high-quality printing equipment. Learn standard envelope formats for business, and retain a copy of every cover letter you send out. You can use the copies to take notes of any telephone conversations that may occur.

If attending a job fair, either carry a briefcase or place your résumé in a nicely covered legal-size pad holder.

The Cover Letter

The cover letter provides you with the opportunity to tailor your résumé by telling the prospective employer how you can be a benefit to the organization. It allows you to highlight aspects of your background that are not already discussed in your résumé and that might be especially relevant to the organization you are contacting or to the position you are seeking. Every résumé should have a cover letter enclosed when you send it out. Unlike the résumé, which may be mass-produced, a cover letter is most effective when it is individually prepared and focused on the particular requirements of the organization in question.

A good cover letter should supplement the résumé and motivate the reader to review the résumé. The format shown in Exhibit 2.3 (see page 34) is only a suggestion to help you decide what information to include in a cover letter.

Begin the cover letter with your street address six lines down from the top. Leave three to five lines between the date and the name of the person to whom you are addressing the cover letter. Make sure you leave one blank line between the salutation and the body of the letter and between paragraphs. After typing "Sincerely," leave four blank lines and type your name. This should leave plenty of room for your signature. A sample cover letter is shown in Exhibit 2.4 on page 35.

The following guidelines will help you write good cover letters:

1. Be sure to type your letter neatly; ensure there are no misspellings.
2. Avoid unusual typefaces, such as script.
3. Address the letter to an individual, using the person's name and title. To obtain this information, call the company. If answering a blind newspaper advertisement, address the letter "To Whom It May Concern" or omit the salutation.
4. Be sure your cover letter directly indicates the position you are applying for and tells why you are qualified to fill it.
5. Send the original letter, not a photocopy, with your résumé. Keep a copy for your records.
6. Make your cover letter no more than one page.
7. Include a phone number where you can be reached.
8. Avoid trite language and have someone read the letter over to react to its tone, content, and mechanics.
9. For your own information, record the date you send out each letter and résumé.

Exhibit 2.3
COVER LETTER FORMAT

Your Street Address
Your Town, State, Zip
Phone Number
Fax Number
E-mail

Date

Name
Title
Organization
Address

Dear _____:

First Paragraph. In this paragraph state the reason for the letter, name the specific position or type of work you are applying for, and indicate from which resource (career services office, website, newspaper, contact, employment service) you learned of this opening. The first paragraph can also be used to inquire about future openings.

Second Paragraph. Indicate why you are interested in this position, the company, or its products or services and what you can do for the employer. If you are a recent graduate, explain how your academic background makes you a qualified candidate. Try not to repeat the same information found in the résumé.

Third Paragraph. Refer the reader to the enclosed résumé for more detailed information.

Fourth Paragraph. In this paragraph say what you will do to follow up on your letter. For example, state that you will call by a certain date to set up an interview or to find out if the company will be recruiting in your area. Finish by indicating your willingness to answer any questions the recipient may have. Be sure you have provided your phone number.

Sincerely,

Type your name

Enclosure

Exhibit 2.4
SAMPLE COVER LETTER

555 S. Main St.
Rochester Hills, MI 48307
(248) 555-1212
ohayfarm@xxx.net

Date

Andrea Phillips
Director of Human Services
Oakland County Office of Social Services
123 Hugo St.
Rochester, MI 48309

Dear Ms. Phillips:

I read of your opening for an independent living counselor on your website, and I am very interested in talking with you about this position. In May 2007 I will graduate from Oakland University with a bachelor of arts degree in psychology.

The job description indicates that you are looking for someone to provide support and teach independent living skills to adults with developmental disabilities, and that a bachelor's degree in psychology is required. The enclosed résumé outlines my educational and work experience. Most recently, I completed a half-year internship at a substance abuse halfway house. This allowed me the opportunity to learn about the variety of records that are maintained for patients and associated insurance coverage. In a volunteer position, I taught independent living skills to women who were leaving abusive partners and trying to make it on their own. My counseling style is still evolving, yet it is characterized by sensitivity and empathy and is solution focused.

Enclosed is a copy of my résumé for your review. It highlights my education and experience.

I hope to meet with you to discuss how my education and experience are consistent with your needs, and how I could become a valued member of your office's team. Next week I will contact you to arrange an interview. In the

continued

meantime, if you require additional information, please contact me using the telephone number or e-mail address listed above.

Sincerely,

Olivia Hayfarmer

Enclosure

3

Researching Careers and Networking

One reason for confusion is perhaps a mistaken assumption that a college education provides job training. In most cases it does not. Of course, applied fields such as engineering, management, or education provide specific skills for the workplace as well as an education.

What Do They Call the Job You Want?

Your overall college education exposes you to numerous fields of study and teaches you quantitative reasoning, critical thinking, writing, and speaking, all of which can be successfully applied to a number of different job fields. But it still remains up to you to choose a job field and to learn how to articulate the benefits of your education in a way the employer will appreciate.

A common question that career counselors encounter from psychology majors is "What can I really do with my degree?" Psychology majors have learned about psychology, but they may not have learned how to put their knowledge to work. Those students earning accounting, computer science, and teaching degrees, just to name a few, have been taught how to begin their careers. Your friend who is a marketing major knows she'll start her career in sales. If you are not sure of the kind of work you are qualified for—or the type of employer that would hire you—this chapter will help you gain that understanding.

Collect Job Titles

The world of employment is a complex place, so you need to become a bit of an explorer and adventurer and be willing to try a variety of techniques to develop a list of possible occupations that might use your talents and education. You might find computerized interest inventories, reference books and other sources, and classified ads helpful in this respect. Once you have a list of possibilities that you are interested in and qualified for, you can move on to find out what kinds of organizations have these job titles.

Computerized Interest Inventories. One way to begin collecting job titles is to identify a number of jobs that call for your degree and the particular skills and interests you identified as part of the self-assessment process. There are excellent interactive career-guidance programs on the market to help you produce such selected lists of possible job titles. Most of these are available at colleges and at some larger town and city libraries. Two of the industry leaders are *CHOICES* and *DISCOVER*. Both allow you to enter interests, values, educational background, and other information to produce lists of possible occupations and industries. Each of the resources listed here will produce different job title lists. Some job titles will appear again and again, while others will be unique to a particular source. Investigate all of them!

Reference Sources. Books on the market that may be available through your local library or career counseling office also suggest various occupations related to specific majors. The following are only a few of the many good books on the market: *College Majors and Careers: A Resource Guide for Effective Life Planning* by Paul Phifer, *Guide to College Majors* by Erik Olson and Lisa M. Rovito, and *College Majors Handbook with Real Career Paths and Payoffs* by Paul Harrington and Thomas Harrington. All of these books list possible job titles within the academic major.

A psychology major interested in community or human services work could consider working at a senior citizens center, in a teen drop-in center, in an area home for battered or abused women, or in a veterans affairs office. The job title might be the same in each situation—counselor. On the other hand, many job titles give you a sense of the job expectations, including such titles as residential clinician-overnight, (geographic)-area counselor, asleep overnight counselor, youth counselor, street outreach counselor, or family counselor. If a job title captures your interests, add it to your list.

Each employer offers a different environment, or "culture," with associated norms in the pace of work, the clients' presenting issues, and the background and training of those you'll be working alongside. Do any of the following seem more attractive to you: not-for-profit social service agency, federal government agency, for-profit health-care agency, county education department, private school, state government agency, or international corporation? As with job titles, look for work environments that are interesting to you.

Each job title deserves your consideration. Like removing the layers of an onion, the search for job titles can go on and on! As you spend time doing this activity, you are actually learning more about the value of your degree. What's important in your search at this point is not to become critical or selective but rather to develop as long a list of possibilities as you can. Every source used will help you add new and potentially exciting jobs to your growing list.

Classified Ads. It has been well publicized that the classified ad section of the newspaper represents only a small fraction of the current job market. Nevertheless, the weekly classified ads can be a great help to you in your search. Although they may not be the best place to look for a job, they can teach you a lot about the job market. Classified ads provide a good education in job descriptions, duties, responsibilities, and qualifications. In addition, they provide insight into which industries are actively recruiting and some indication of the area's employment market. This is particularly helpful when seeking a position in a specific geographic area and/or a specific field. For your purposes, classified ads are a good source for job titles to add to your list.

Read the Sunday classified ads in a major market newspaper for several weeks in a row. Cut and paste all the ads that interest you and seem to call for something close to your education, skills, experience, and interests. Remember that classified ads are written for what an organization *hopes* to find; you don't have to meet absolutely every criterion. However, if certain requirements are stated as absolute minimums and you cannot meet them, it's best not to waste your time and that of the employer.

The weekly classified want ads exercise is important because these jobs are out in the marketplace. They truly exist, and people with your qualifications are being sought to apply. What's more, many of these advertisements describe the duties and responsibilities of the job advertised and give you a beginning sense of the challenges and opportunities such a position presents.

Some will indicate salary, and that will be helpful as well. This information will better define the jobs for you and provide some good material for possible interviews in that field.

Explore Job Descriptions

Once you've arrived at a solid list of possible job titles that interest you and for which you believe you are somewhat qualified, it's a good idea to do some research on each of these jobs. The preeminent source for such job information is the *Dictionary of Occupational Titles*, or *DOT* (http://online.onet center.org). This directory lists every conceivable job and provides excellent up-to-date information on duties and responsibilities, interactions with associates, and day-to-day assignments and tasks. These descriptions provide a thorough job analysis, but they do not consider the possible employers or the environments in which a job may be performed. So, although a position as public relations officer may be well defined in terms of duties and responsibilities, it does not explain the differences in doing public relations work in a college or a hospital or a factory or a bank. You will need to look somewhere else for work settings.

Learn More About Possible Work Settings

After reading some job descriptions, you may choose to edit and revise your list of job titles once again, discarding those you feel are not suitable and keeping those that continue to hold your interest. Or you may wish to keep your list intact and see where these jobs may be located. For example, if you are interested in public relations and you appear to have those skills and the requisite education, you'll want to know which organizations do public relations. How can you find that out? How much income does someone in public relations make a year and what is the employment potential for the field of public relations?

To answer these and many other questions about your list of job titles, we recommend you try any of the following resources: *Careers Encyclopedia*, the professional societies and resources found throughout this book, *College to Career: The Guide to Job Opportunities*, and the *Occupational Outlook Handbook* (http://stats.bls.gov/ocohome.htm). Each of these resources, in a different way, will help to put the job titles you have selected into an employer context. Perhaps the most extensive discussion is found in the *Occupational Outlook Handbook*, which gives a thorough presentation of the nature of the work, the working conditions, employment statistics, training, other qualifications, and advancement possibilities as well as job outlook and earnings. Related occupations are also detailed, and a select bibliography is provided to help you find additional information.

Continuing with our public relations example, your search through these reference materials would teach you that the public relations jobs you find attractive are available in larger hospitals, financial institutions, most corporations (both consumer goods and industrial goods), media organizations, and colleges and universities.

Networking

Networking is the process of deliberately establishing relationships to get career-related information or to alert potential employers that you are available for work. Networking is critically important to today's job seeker for two reasons: it will help you get the information you need, and it can help you find out about *all* of the available jobs.

Get the Information You Need

Networkers will review your résumé and give you feedback on its effectiveness. They will talk about the job you are looking for and give you a candid appraisal of how they see your strengths and weaknesses. If they have a good sense of the industry or the employment sector for that job, you'll get their feelings on future trends in the industry as well. Some networkers will be very forthcoming about salaries, job-hunting techniques, and suggestions for your job search strategy. Many have been known to place calls right from the interview desk to friends and associates who might be interested in you. Each networker will make his or her own contribution, and each will be valuable.

Because organizations must evolve to adapt to current global market needs, the information provided by decision makers within various organizations will be critical to your success as a new job market entrant. For example, you might learn about the concept of virtual organizations from a networker. Virtual organizations coordinate economic activity to deliver value to customers by using resources outside the traditional boundaries of the organization. This concept is being discussed and implemented by chief executive officers of many organizations, including Ford Motor, Dell, and IBM. Networking can help you find out about this and other trends currently affecting the industries under your consideration.

Find Out About All of the Available Jobs

Not every job that is available at this very moment is advertised for potential applicants to see. This is called the *hidden job market*. Only 15 to 20 percent of all jobs are formally advertised, which means that 80 to 85 percent of available jobs do not appear in published channels. Networking will help you become more knowledgeable about all the employment opportunities available during your job search period.

Although someone you might talk to today doesn't know of any openings within his or her organization, tomorrow or next week or next month an opening may occur. If you've taken the time to show an interest in and knowledge of their organization, if you've shown the company representative how you can help achieve organizational goals and that you can fit into the organization, you'll be one of the first candidates considered for the position.

Networking: A Proactive Approach

Networking is a proactive rather than a reactive approach. You, as a job seeker, are expected to initiate a certain level of activity on your own behalf; you cannot afford to simply respond to jobs listed in the newspaper. Being proactive means building a network of contacts that includes informed and interested decision makers who will provide you with up-to-date knowledge of the current job market and increase your chances of finding out about employment opportunities appropriate for your interests, experience, and level of education. An old axiom of networking says, "You are only two phone calls away from the information you need." In other words, by talking to enough people, you will quickly come across someone who can offer you help.

Preparing to Network

In deliberately establishing relationships, maximize your efforts by organizing your approach. Five specific areas in which you can organize your efforts include reviewing your self-assessment, reviewing your research on job sites and organizations, deciding who you want to talk to, keeping track of all your efforts, and creating your self-promotion tools.

Review Your Self-Assessment

Your self-assessment is as important a tool in preparing to network as it has been in other aspects of your job search. You have carefully evaluated your personal traits, personal values, economic needs, longer-term goals, skill base, preferred skills, and underdeveloped skills. During the networking process you will be called upon to communicate what you know about yourself and relate it to the information or job you seek. Be sure to review the exercises that you completed in the self-assessment section of this book in preparation for networking. We've explained that you need to assess which skills you have acquired from your major that are of general value to an employer; be ready to express those in ways he or she can appreciate as useful in the organizations.

Review Research on Job Sites and Organizations

In addition, individuals assisting you will expect that you'll have at least some background information on the occupation or industry of interest to you. Refer to the appropriate sections of this book and other relevant publications to acquire the background information necessary for effective networking. They'll explain how to identify not only the job titles that might be of interest to you but also which kinds of organizations employ people to do that job. You will develop some sense of working conditions and expectations about duties and responsibilities—all of which will be of help in your networking interviews.

Decide Who You Want to Talk To

Networking cannot begin until you decide who you want to talk to and, in general, what type of information you hope to gain from your contacts. Once you know this, it's time to begin developing a list of contacts. Five useful sources for locating contacts are described here.

College Alumni Network. Most colleges and universities have created a formal network of alumni and friends of the institution who are particularly interested in helping currently enrolled students and graduates of their alma mater gain employment-related information.

It is usually a simple process to make use of an alumni network. Visit your college's website and locate the alumni office and/or your career center. Either or both sites will have information about your school's alumni network. You'll be provided with information on shadowing experiences, geographic information, or those alumni offering job referrals. If you don't find what you're looking for, don't hesitate to phone or e-mail your career center and ask what they can do to help you connect with an alum.

Alumni networkers may provide some combination of the following services: day-long shadowing experiences, telephone interviews, in-person interviews, information on relocating to given geographic areas, internship information, suggestions on graduate school study, and job vacancy notices.

Present and Former Supervisors. If you believe you are on good terms with present or former job supervisors, they may be an excellent resource for providing information or directing you to appropriate resources that would have information related to your current interests and needs. Additionally, these supervisors probably belong to professional organizations that they might be willing to utilize to get information for you.

Employers in Your Area. Although you may be interested in working in a geographic location different from the one where you currently reside, don't overlook the value of the knowledge and contacts those around you are able to provide. Use the local telephone directory and newspaper to identify the types of organizations you are thinking of working for or professionals who have the kinds of jobs you are interested in. Recently, a call made to a local hospital's financial administrator for information on working in health-care financial administration yielded more pertinent information on training seminars, regional professional organizations, and potential employment sites than a national organization was willing to provide.

Employers in Geographic Areas Where You Hope to Work. If you are thinking about relocating, identifying prospective employers or informational contacts in the new location will be critical to your success. Here are some tips for online searching. First, use a "metasearch" engine to get the most out of your search. Metasearch engines combine several engines into one powerful tool. We frequently use dogpile.com and metasearch.com for this purpose. Try using the city and state as your keywords in a search. *New Haven, Connecticut* will bring you to the city's website with links to the chamber of commerce, member businesses, and other valuable resources. By using looksmart.com you can locate newspapers in any area, and they, too, can provide valuable insight before you relocate. Of course, both dogpile and metasearch can lead you to yellow and white page directories in areas you are considering.

Professional Associations and Organizations. Professional associations and organizations can provide valuable information in several areas: career paths that you might not have considered, qualifications relating to those career choices, publications that list current job openings, and workshops or seminars that will enhance your professional knowledge and skills. They can also be excellent sources for background information on given industries: their health, current problems, and future challenges.

There are several excellent resources available to help you locate professional associations and organizations that would have information to meet your needs. Two especially useful publications are the *Encyclopedia of Associations* and *National Trade and Professional Associations of the United States*.

Keep Track of All Your Efforts

It can be difficult, almost impossible, to remember all the details related to each contact you make during the networking process, so you will want to develop a record-keeping system that works for you. Formalize this process by using your computer to keep a record of the people and organizations you want to contact. You can simply record the contact's name, address, and telephone number, and what information you hope to gain.

You could record this as a simple Word document and you could still use the "Find" function if you were trying to locate some data and could only recall the firm's name or the contact's name. If you're comfortable with database management and you have some database software on your computer, then you can put information at your fingertips even if you have only the zip code! The point here is not technological sophistication but good record keeping.

Once you have created this initial list, it will be helpful to keep more detailed information as you begin to actually make the contacts. Those details should include complete contact information, the date and content of each contact, names and information for additional networkers, and required follow-up. Don't forget to send a letter thanking your contact for his or her time! Your contact will appreciate your recall of details of your meetings and conversations, and the information will help you to focus your networking efforts.

Create Your Self-Promotion Tools

There are two types of promotional tools that are used in the networking process. The first is a résumé and cover letter, and the second is a one-minute "infomercial," which may be given over the telephone or in person.

Techniques for writing an effective résumé and cover letter are discussed in Chapter 2. Once you have reviewed that material and prepared these important documents, you will have created one of your self-promotion tools.

The one-minute infomercial will demand that you begin tying your interests, abilities, and skills to the people or organizations you want to network with. Think about your goal for making the contact to help you understand what you should say about yourself. You should be able to express yourself easily and convincingly. If, for example, you are contacting an alumnus of your institution to obtain the names of possible employment sites in a distant city, be prepared to discuss why you are interested in moving to that location, the types of jobs you are interested in, and the skills and abilities you possess that will make you a qualified candidate.

To create a meaningful one-minute infomercial, write it out, practice it as if it will be a spoken presentation, rewrite it, and practice it again if necessary until expressing yourself comes easily and is convincing.

Here's a simplified example of an infomercial for use over the telephone:

Hello, Mr. Smith? My name is Olivia Hayfarmer. I am a recent graduate of Oakland University, and I hope to pursue a counseling career. My major was psychology, and I feel I've developed entry-level skills valued in the helping profession, such as empathic listening, thoughtful and clear feedback based on sound psychological principles, and accurate and thorough post-session record keeping. I also know that I'm calm when facing crisis situations.

Mr. Smith, I'm calling you because I still need more information about working as a counselor and one of my professors recommended that I talk with you. I'm hoping you'll have time to meet with me for about half an hour to discuss your perspective on counseling careers. There are so many types of jobs and employers, and I'm seeking advice on the options that would best fit my combination of skills and experience.

Would you be willing to meet with me? I am available any afternoon after 1:00, if that would work for you.

It very well may happen that your employer contact wishes you to communicate by e-mail. The infomercial quoted above could easily be rewritten for an e-mail message. You should "cut and paste" your résumé right into the e-mail text itself.

Other effective self-promotion tools include portfolios for those in the arts, writing professions, or teaching. Portfolios show examples of work, photographs of projects or classroom activities, or certificates and credentials that are job related. There may not be an opportunity to use the portfolio during an interview, and it is not something that should be left with the organization. It is designed to be explained and displayed by the creator. However, during some networking meetings, there may be an opportunity to illustrate a point or strengthen a qualification by exhibiting the portfolio.

Beginning the Networking Process

Set the Tone for Your Communications

It can be useful to establish "tone words" for any communications you embark upon. Before making your first telephone call or writing your first letter, decide what you want the person to think of you. If you are networking to try to obtain a job, your tone words might include descriptors such as *genuine, informed,* and *self-knowledgeable*. When you're trying to acquire information, your tone words may have a slightly different focus, such as *courteous, organized, focused,* and *well-spoken*. Use the tone words you establish for your contacts to guide you through the networking process.

Honestly Express Your Intentions

When contacting individuals, it is important to be honest about your reasons for making the contact. Establish your purpose in your own mind and be able and ready to articulate it concisely. Determine an initial agenda, whether it be informational questioning or self-promotion, present it to your contact, and be ready to respond immediately. If you don't adequately prepare before initiating your overture, you may find yourself at a disadvantage if you're asked to immediately begin your informational interview or self-promotion during the first phone conversation or visit.

Start Networking Within Your Circle of Confidence

Once you have organized your approach—by utilizing specific researching methods, creating a system for keeping track of the people you will contact, and developing effective self-promotion tools—you are ready to begin networking. The best way to begin networking is by talking with a group of people you trust and feel comfortable with. This group is usually made up of your family, friends, and career counselors. No matter who is in this inner circle, they will have a special interest in seeing you succeed in your job search. In addition, because they will be easy to talk to, you should try taking some risks in terms of practicing your information-seeking approach. Gain confidence in talking about the strengths you bring to an organization and the underdeveloped skills you feel hinder your candidacy. Be sure to review the section on self-assessment for tips on approaching each of these areas. Ask for critical but constructive feedback from the people in your circle of confidence on the letters you write and the one-minute infomercial you have developed. Evaluate whether you want to make the changes they suggest, then practice the changes on others within this circle.

Stretch the Boundaries of Your Networking Circle of Confidence

Once you have refined the promotional tools you will use to accomplish your networking goals, you will want to make additional contacts. Because you will not know most of these people, it will be a less comfortable activity to undertake. The practice that you gained with your inner circle of trusted friends should have prepared you to now move outside of that comfort zone.

It is said that any information a person needs is only two phone calls away, but the information cannot be gained until you (1) make a reasonable guess about who might have the information you need and (2) pick up the telephone to make the call. Using your network list that includes alumni, instructors, supervisors, employers, and associations, you can begin preparing your list of questions that will allow you to get the information you need.

Prepare the Questions You Want to Ask

Networkers can provide you with the insider's perspective on any given field and you can ask them questions that you might not want to ask in an interview. For example, you can ask them to describe the more repetitious or mundane parts of the job or ask them for a realistic idea of salary expectations. Be sure to prepare your questions ahead of time so that you are organized and efficient.

Be Prepared to Answer Some Questions

To communicate effectively, you must anticipate questions that will be asked of you by the networkers you contact. Revisit the self-assessment process you undertook and the research you've done so that you can effortlessly respond to questions about your short- and long-term goals and the kinds of jobs you are most interested in pursuing.

General Networking Tips

Make Every Contact Count. Setting the tone for each interaction is critical. Approaches that will help you communicate in an effective way include politeness, being appreciative of time provided to you, and being prepared and thorough. Remember, *everyone* within an organization has a circle of influence, so be prepared to interact effectively with each person you encounter in the networking process, including secretarial and support staff. Many information or job seekers have thwarted their own efforts by being rude to some individuals they encountered as they networked because they made the incorrect assumption that certain persons were unimportant.

Sometimes your contacts may be surprised at their ability to help you. After meeting and talking with you, they might think they have not offered much in the way of help. A day or two later, however, they may make a contact that would be useful to you and refer you to that person.

With Each Contact, Widen Your Circle of Networkers. Always leave an informational interview with the names of at least two more people who can help you get the information or job that you are seeking. Don't be shy about asking for additional contacts; networking is all about increasing the number of people you can interact with to achieve your goals.

Make Your Own Decisions. As you talk with different people and get answers to the questions you pose, you may hear conflicting information or get conflicting suggestions. Your job is to listen to these "experts" and decide what information and which suggestions will help you achieve *your* goals. Only implement those suggestions that you believe will work for you.

Shutting Down Your Network

As you achieve the goals that motivated your networking activity—getting the information you need or the job you want—the time will come to inactivate all or parts of your network. As you do, be sure to tell your primary supporters about your change in status. Call or write to each one of them and give them as many details about your new status as you feel is necessary to maintain a positive relationship.

Because a network takes on a life of its own, activity undertaken on your behalf will continue even after you cease your efforts. As you get calls or are contacted in some fashion, be sure to inform these networkers about your change in status, and thank them for assistance they have provided.

Information on the latest employment trends indicates that workers will change jobs or careers several times in their lifetime. Networking, then, will be a critical aspect in the span of your professional life. If you carefully and thoughtfully conduct your networking activities during your job search, you will have a solid foundation of experience when you need to network the next time around.

Where Are These Jobs, Anyway?

Having a list of job titles that you've designed around your own career interests and skills is an excellent beginning. It means you've really thought about who you are and what you are presenting to the employment market. It has caused you to think seriously about the most appealing environments to work in, and you have identified some employer types that represent these environments.

The research and the thinking that you've done thus far will be used again and again. They will be helpful in writing your résumé and cover letters, in talking about yourself on the telephone to prospective employers, and in answering interview questions.

Now is a good time to begin to narrow the field of job titles and employment sites down to some specific employers to initiate the employment contact.

Find Out Which Employers Hire People Like You

This section will provide tips, techniques, and specific resources for developing an actual list of specific employers that can be used to make contacts. It is only an outline that you must be prepared to tailor to your own particular needs and according to what you bring to the job search. Once again, it is important to communicate with others along the way exactly what you're looking for and what your goals are for the research you're doing. Librarians, employers, career counselors, friends, friends of friends, business contacts, and bookstore staff will all have helpful information on geographically specific and new resources to aid you in locating employers who'll hire you.

Identify Information Resources

Your interview wardrobe and your new résumé might have put a dent in your wallet, but the resources you'll need to pursue your job search are available for free. The categories of information detailed here are not hard to find and are yours for the browsing.

Numerous resources described in this section will help you identify actual employers. Use all of them or any others that you identify as available in your geographic area. As you become experienced in this pro figure out which information sources are helpful and which a. live in a rural area, a well-planned day trip to a major city that incluc college career office, a large college or city library, state and federal employment centers, a chamber of commerce office, and a well-stocked bookstore can produce valuable results.

There are many excellent resources available to help you identify actual job sites. They are categorized into employer directories (usually indexed by product lines and geographic location), geographically based directories (designed to highlight particular cities, regions, or states), career-specific directories (e.g., *Sports MarketPlace*, which lists tens of thousands of firms involved with sports), periodicals and newspapers, targeted job posting publications, and videos. This is by no means meant to be a complete treatment of resources but rather a starting point for identifying useful resources.

Working from the more general references to highly specific resources, we provide a basic list to help you begin your search. Many of these you'll find easily available. In some cases reference librarians and others will suggest even better materials for your particular situation. Start to create your own customized bibliography of job search references.

Geographically Based Directories. The Job Bank series published by Bob Adams, Inc. (aip.com) contains detailed entries on each area's major employers, including business activity, address, phone number, and hiring contact name. Many listings specify educational backgrounds being sought in potential employees. Each volume contains a solid discussion of each city's or state's major employment sectors. Organizations are also indexed by industry. Job Bank volumes are available for the following places: Atlanta, Boston, Chicago, Dallas–Ft. Worth, Denver, Detroit, Florida, Houston, Los Angeles, Minneapolis, New York, Ohio, Philadelphia, San Francisco, Seattle, St. Louis, Washington, D.C., and other cities throughout the Northwest.

National Job Bank (careercity.com) lists employers in every state, along with contact names and commonly hired job categories. Included are many small companies often overlooked by other directories. Companies are also indexed by industry. This publication provides information on educational backgrounds sought and lists company benefits.

Periodicals and Newspapers. Several sources are available to help you locate which journals or magazines carry job advertisements in your field. Other resources help you identify opportunities in other parts of the country.

- *Where the Jobs Are: A Comprehensive Directory of 1200 Journals Listing Career Opportunities*
- *Corptech Fast 5000 Company Locator*
- *National Ad Search* (nationaladsearch.com)
- *The Federal Jobs Digest* (jobsfed.com) and *Federal Career Opportunities*
- *World Chamber of Commerce Directory* (chamberofcommerce.org)

This list is certainly not exhaustive; use it to begin your job search work.

Targeted Job Posting Publications. Although the resources that follow are national in scope, they are either targeted to one medium of contact (telephone), focused on specific types of jobs, or less comprehensive than the sources previously listed.

- Careers.org (careers.org/index.html)
- *The Job Hunter* (jobhunter.com)
- *Current Jobs for Graduates* (graduatejobs.com)
- *Environmental Opportunities* (ecojobs.com)
- *Y National Vacancy List* (ymca.net/employment/ymca_recruiting/jobright.htm)
- *ArtSEARCH*
- *Community Jobs*
- *National Association of Colleges and Employers: Job Choices series*
- *National Association of Colleges and Employers* (jobweb.com)

Videos. You may be one of the many job seekers who likes to get information via a medium other than paper. Many career libraries, public libraries, and career centers in libraries carry an assortment of videos that will help you learn new techniques and get information helpful in the job search.

Locate Information Resources

Throughout these introductory chapters, we have continually referred you to various websites for information on everything from job listings to career information. Using the Web gives you a mobility at your computer that you don't enjoy if you rely solely on books or newspapers or printed journals. Moreover, material on the Web, if the site is maintained, can be the most up-to-date information available.

You'll eventually identify the information resources that work best for you, but make certain you've covered the full range of resources before you begin to rely on a smaller list. Here's a short list of informational sites that many job seekers find helpful:

- Public and college libraries
- College career centers
- Bookstores
- The Internet
- Local and state government personnel offices
- Career/job fairs

Each one of these sites offers a collection of resources that will help you get the information you need.

As you meet and talk with service professionals at all these sites, be sure to let them know what you're doing. Inform them of your job search, what you've already accomplished, and what you're looking for. The more people who know you're job seeking, the greater the possibility that someone will have information or know someone who can help you along your way.

4

Interviewing and Job Offer Considerations

Certainly, there can be no one part of the job search process more fraught with anxiety and worry than the interview. Yet seasoned job seekers welcome the interview and will often say, "Just get me an interview and I'm on my way!" They understand that the interview is crucial to the hiring process and equally crucial for them, as job candidates, to have the opportunity of a personal dialogue to add to what the employer may already have learned from the résumé, cover letter, and telephone conversations.

Believe it or not, the interview is to be welcomed, and even enjoyed! It is a perfect opportunity for you, the candidate, to sit down with an employer and express yourself and display who you are and what you want. Of course, it takes thought and planning and a little strategy; after all, it *is* a job interview! But it can be a positive, if not pleasant, experience and one you can look back on and feel confident about your performance and effort.

For many new job seekers, a job, any job, seems a wonderful thing. But seasoned interview veterans know that the job interview is an important step for both sides—the employer and the candidate—to see what each has to offer and whether there is going to be a "fit" of personalities, work styles, and attitudes. And it is this concept of balance in the interview, that both sides have important parts to play, that holds the key to success in mastering this aspect of the job search strategy.

Try to think of the interview as a conversation between two interested and equal partners. You both have important, even vital, information to deliver and to learn. Of course, there's no denying the employer has some leverage, especially in the initial interview for recruitment or any interview scheduled by the candidate and not the recruiter. That should not prevent the interviewee from seeking to play an equal part in what should be a fair exchange of information. Too often the untutored candidate allows the interview to become one-sided. The employer asks all the questions and the candidate simply responds. The ideal would be for two mutually interested parties to sit down and discuss possibilities for each. This is a conversation of significance, and it requires preparation, thought about the tone of the interview, and planning of the nature and details of the information to be exchanged.

Preparing for the Interview

The length of most initial interviews is about thirty minutes. Given the brevity, the information that is exchanged ought to be important. The candidate should be delivering material that the employer cannot discover on the résumé, and in turn, the candidate should be learning things about the employer that he or she could not otherwise find out. After all, if you have only thirty minutes, why waste time on information that is already published? The information exchanged is more than just factual, and both sides will learn much from what they see of each other, as well. How the candidate looks, speaks, and acts are important to the employer. The employer's attention to the interview and awareness of the candidate's résumé, the setting, and the quality of information presented are important to the candidate.

Just as the employer has every right to be disappointed when a prospect is late for the interview, looks unkempt, and seems ill-prepared to answer fairly standard questions, the candidate may be disappointed with an interviewer who isn't ready for the meeting, hasn't learned the basic résumé facts, and is constantly interrupted by telephone calls. In either situation there's good reason to feel let down.

There are many elements to a successful interview, and some of them are not easy to describe or prepare for. Sometimes there is just a chemistry between interviewer and interviewee that brings out the best in both, and a good exchange takes place. But there is much the candidate can do to pave the way for success in terms of his or her résumé, personal appearance, goals, and interview strategy—each of which we will discuss. However, none of this preparation is as important as the time and thought the candidate gives to personal self-assessment.

Self-Assessment
Neither a stunning résumé nor an expensive, well-tailored suit can compensate for candidates who do not know what they want, where they are going, or why they are interviewing with a particular employer. Self-assessment, the

process by which we begin to know and acknowledge our own particular blend of education, experiences, needs, and goals, is not something that can be sorted out the weekend before a major interview. Of all the elements of interview preparation, this one requires the longest lead time and cannot be faked.

Because the time allotted for most interviews is brief, it is all the more important for job candidates to understand and express succinctly why they are there and what they have to offer. This is not a time for undue modesty (or for braggadocio either); it is a time for a compelling, reasoned statement of why you feel that you and this employer might make a good match. It means you have to have thought about your skills, interests, and attributes; related those to your life experiences and your own history of challenges and opportunities; and determined what that indicates about your strengths, preferences, values, and areas needing further development.

If you need some assistance with self-assessment issues, refer to Chapter 1. Included are suggested exercises that can be done as needed, such as making up an experiential diary and extracting obvious strengths and weaknesses from past experiences. These simple assignments will help you look at past activities as collections of tasks with accompanying skills and responsibilities. Don't overlook your high school or college career office. Many offer personal counseling on self-assessment issues and may provide testing instruments such as the *Myers-Briggs Type Indicator (MBTI)*, the *Harrington-O'Shea Career Decision-Making System (CDM)*, the *Strong Interest Inventory (SII)*, or any other of a wide selection of assessment tools that can help you clarify some of these issues prior to the interview stage of your job search.

The Résumé

Résumé preparation has been discussed in detail, and some basic examples were provided. In this section we want to concentrate on how best to use your résumé in the interview. In most cases the employer will have seen the résumé prior to the interview, and, in fact, it may well have been the quality of that résumé that secured the interview opportunity.

An interview is a conversation, however, and not an exercise in reading. So, if the employer hasn't seen your résumé and you have brought it along to the interview, wait until asked or until the end of the interview to offer it. Otherwise, you may find yourself staring at the back of your résumé and simply answering "yes" and "no" to a series of questions drawn from that document.

Sometimes an interviewer is not prepared and does not know or recall the contents of the résumé and may use the résumé to a greater or lesser degree as a "prompt" during the interview. It is for you to judge what that may indicate about the individual performing the interview or the employer. If your interviewer seems surprised by the scheduled meeting, relies on the résumé to an inordinate degree, and seems otherwise unfamiliar with your background, this lack of preparation for the hiring process could well be a symptom of general management disorganization or may simply be the result of poor planning on the part of one individual. It is your responsibility as a potential employee to be aware of these signals and make your decisions accordingly.

If you find that the interviewer is reading from your résumé rather than discussing the job with you, you can guide the interviewer back to the job dialogue by saying, "Mr. Davis, I would like to elaborate on the experience I gained in an internship that is not detailed on my résumé." This strategy may give you an opportunity to convey more information about your strengths and weaknesses and will reengage the direction of your interview.

By all means, bring at least one copy of your résumé to the interview. Occasionally, at the close of an interview, an interviewer will express an interest in circulating a résumé to several departments, and you could then offer the copy you brought. Sometimes, an interview appointment provides an opportunity to meet others in the organization who may express an interest in you and your background, and it may be helpful to follow up with a copy of your résumé. Our best advice, however, is to keep it out of sight until needed or requested.

Employer Information

Whether your interview is for graduate school admission, an overseas corporate position, or a position with a local company, it is important to know something about the employer or the organization. Keeping in mind that the interview is relatively brief and that you will hopefully have other interviews with other organizations, it is important to keep your research in proportion. If secondary interviews are called for, you will have additional time to do further research. For the first interview, it is helpful to know the organization's mission, goals, size, scope of operations, and so forth. Your research may uncover recent areas of challenge or particular successes that may help to fuel the interview. Use the "What Do They Call the Job You Want?" section of Chapter 3, your library, and your career or guidance office to help you locate this information in the most efficient way possible. Don't be shy in asking advice of these counseling and guidance professionals on how best to spend your preparation time. With some practice, you'll soon learn how much information is enough and which kinds of information are most useful to you.

Interview Content

We've already discussed how it can help to think of the interview as an important conversation—one that, as with any conversation, you want to find pleasant and interesting and to leave you with a good feeling. But because this conversation is especially important, the information that's exchanged is critical to its success. What do you want them to know about you? What do you need to know about them? What interview technique do you need to particularly pay attention to? How do you want to manage the close of the interview? What steps will follow in the hiring process?

Except for the professional interviewer, most of us find interviewing stressful and anxiety-provoking. Developing a strategy before you begin interviewing will help you relieve some stress and anxiety. One particular strategy that has worked for many and may work for you is interviewing by objective. Before you interview, write down three to five goals you would like to achieve for that interview. They may be technique goals: smile a little more, have a firmer handshake, be sure to ask about the next stage in the interview process before leaving. They may be content-oriented goals: find out about the company's current challenges and opportunities; be sure to speak of your recent research, writing experiences, or foreign travel. Whatever your goals, jot down a few of them as goals for each interview.

Most people find that in trying to achieve these few goals, their interviewing technique becomes more organized and focused. After the interview, the most common question friends and family ask is "How did it go?" With this technique, you have an indication of whether you met *your* goals for the meeting, not just some vague idea of how it went. Chances are, if you accomplished what you wanted to, it improved the quality of the entire interview. As you continue to interview, you will want to revise your goals to continue improving your interview skills.

Now, add to the concept of the significant conversation the idea of a beginning, a middle, and a closing and you will have two thoughts that will give your interview a distinctive character. Be sure to make your introduction warm and cordial. Say your full name (and if it's a difficult-to-pronounce name, help the interviewer to pronounce it) and make certain you know your interviewer's name and how to pronounce it. Most interviews begin with some "soft talk" about the weather, chat about the candidate's trip to the interview site, or national events. This is done as a courtesy to relax both you and the interviewer, to get you talking, and to generally try to defuse the atmosphere of excessive tension. Try to be yourself, engage in the conversation, and don't try to second-guess the interviewer. This is simply what it appears to be—casual conversation.

Once you and the interviewer move on to exchange more serious information in the middle part of the interview, the two most important concerns become your ability to handle challenging questions and your success at asking meaningful ones. Interviewer questions will probably fall into one of three categories: personal assessment and career direction, academic assessment, and knowledge of the employer. Here are a few examples of questions in each category:

Personal Assessment and Career Direction
1. What motivates you to put forth your best effort?
2. What do you consider to be your greatest strengths and weaknesses?
3. What qualifications do you have that make you think you will be successful in this career?

Academic Assessment
1. What led you to choose your major?
2. What subjects did you like best and least? Why?
3. How has your college experience prepared you for this career?

Knowledge of the Employer
1. What do you think it takes to be successful in an organization like ours?
2. In what ways do you think you can make a contribution to our organization?
3. Why did you choose to seek a position with this organization?

The interviewer wants a response to each question but is also gauging your enthusiasm, preparedness, and willingness to communicate. In each response you should provide some information about yourself that can be related to the employer's needs. A common mistake is to give too much information. Answer each question completely, but be careful not to run on too long with extensive details or examples.

Questions About Underdeveloped Skills

Most employers interview people who have met some minimum criteria of education and experience. They interview candidates to see who they are, to learn what kind of personality they exhibit, and to get some sense of how they might fit into the existing organization. It may be that you are asked about skills the employer hopes to find and that you have not documented. Maybe it's grant-writing experience, knowledge of the European political system, or a knowledge of the film world.

To questions about skills and experiences you don't have, answer honestly and forthrightly and try to offer some additional information about skills you do have. For example, perhaps the employer is disappointed you have no grant-writing experience. An honest answer may be as follows:

No, unfortunately, I was never in a position to acquire those skills. I do understand something of the complexities of the grant-writing process and feel confident that my attention to detail, careful reading skills, and strong writing would make grants a wonderful challenge in a new job. I think I could get up on the learning curve quickly.

The employer hears an honest admission of lack of experience but is reassured by some specific skill details that do relate to grant writing and a confident manner that suggests enthusiasm and interest in a challenge.

For many students, questions about their possible contribution to an employer's organization can prove challenging. Because your education has probably not included specific training for a job, you need to review your academic record and select capabilities you have developed in your major that an employer can appreciate. For example, perhaps you read well and can analyze and condense what you've read into smaller, more focused pieces. That could be valuable. Or maybe you did some serious research and you know you have valuable investigative skills. Your public speaking might be highly developed and you might use visual aids appropriately and effectively. Or maybe your skill at correspondence, memos, and messages is effective. Whatever it is, you must take it out of the academic context and put it into a new, employer-friendly context so your interviewer can best judge how you could help the organization.

Exhibiting knowledge of the organization will, without a doubt, show the interviewer that you are interested enough in the available position to have done some legwork in preparation for the interview. Remember, it is not necessary to know every detail of the organization's history but rather to have a general knowledge about why it is in business and how the industry is faring.

Sometime during the interview, generally after the midway point, you'll be asked if you have any questions for the interviewer. Your questions will tell the employer much about your attitude and your desire to understand the organization's expectations so you can compare them to your own strengths. The following are just a few questions you might want to ask:

1. What is the communication style of the organization? (meetings, memos, and so forth)
2. What would a typical day in this position be like for me?
3. What have been some of the interesting challenges and opportunities your organization has recently faced?

Most interviews draw to a natural closing point, so be careful not to prolong the discussion. At a signal from the interviewer, wind up your presentation, express your appreciation for the opportunity, and be sure to ask what the next stage in the process will be. When can you expect to hear from them? Will they be conducting second-tier interviews? If you are interested and haven't heard, would they mind a phone call? Be sure to collect a business card with the name and phone number of your interviewer. On your way out, you might have an opportunity to pick up organizational literature you haven't seen before.

With the right preparation—a thorough self-assessment, professional clothing, and employer information—you'll be able to set and achieve the goals you have established for the interview process.

Interview Follow-Up

Quite often there is a considerable time lag between interviewing for a position and being hired or, in the case of the networker, between your phone call or letter to a possible contact and the opportunity of a meeting. This can be frustrating. "Why aren't they contacting me?" "I thought I'd get another interview, but no one has telephoned." "Am I out of the running?" You don't know what is happening.

Consider the Differing Perspectives

Of course, there is another perspective—that of the networker or hiring organization. Organizations are complex, with multiple tasks that need to be accomplished each day. Hiring is a discrete activity that does not occur as frequently as other job assignments. The hiring process might have to take second place to other, more immediate organizational needs. Although it may be very important to you, and it is certainly ultimately significant to the employer, other issues such as fiscal management, planning and product development, employer vacation periods, or financial constraints may prevent an organization or individual within that organization from acting on your employment or your request for information as quickly as you or they would prefer.

Use Your Communications Skills

Good communication is essential here to resolve any anxieties, and the responsibility is on you, the job or information seeker. Too many job seekers and networkers offer as an excuse that they don't want to "bother" the organization by writing letters or calling. Let us assure you here and now, once and for all, that if you are troubling an organization by over-communicating, someone will indicate that situation to you quite clearly. If not, you can only assume you are a worthwhile prospect and the employer appreciates being reminded of your availability and interest. Let's look at follow-up practices in the job interview process and the networking situation separately.

Following Up on the Employment Interview

A brief thank-you note following an interview is an excellent and polite way to begin a series of follow-up communications with a potential employer with whom you have interviewed and want to remain in touch. It should be just that—a thank-you for a good meeting. If you failed to mention some fact or experience during your interview that you think might add to your candidacy, you may use this note to do that. However, this should be essentially a note whose overall tone is appreciative and, if appropriate, indicative of a continuing interest in pursuing any opportunity that may exist with that organization. It is one of the few pieces of business correspondence that may be handwritten, but always use plain, good-quality, standard-size paper.

If, however, at this point you are no longer interested in the employer, the thank-you note is an appropriate time to indicate that. You are under no obligation to identify any reason for not continuing to pursue employment with that organization, but if you are so inclined to indicate your professional reasons (pursuing other employers more akin to your interests, looking for greater income production than this employer can provide, a different geographic location), you certainly may. It should not be written with an eye to negotiation, for it will not be interpreted as such.

As part of your interview closing, you should have taken the initiative to establish lines of communication for continuing information about your candidacy. If you asked permission to telephone, wait a week following your thank-you note, then telephone your contact simply to inquire how things are progressing on your employment status. The feedback you receive here should be taken at face value. If your interviewer simply has no information, he or she will tell you so and indicate whether you should call again and when. Don't be discouraged if this should continue over some period of time.

If during this time something occurs that you think improves or changes your candidacy (some new qualification or experience you may have had), including any offers from other organizations, by all means telephone or write to inform the employer about this. In the case of an offer from a competing but less desirable or equally desirable organization, telephone your contact, explain what has happened, express your real interest in the organization, and inquire whether some determination on your employment might be made before you must respond to this other offer. An organization that is truly interested in you may be moved to make a decision about your candidacy. Equally possible is the scenario in which they are not yet ready to make a decision and so advise you to take the offer that has been presented. Again, you have no ethical alternative but to deal with the information presented in a straightforward manner.

When accepting other employment, be sure to contact any employers still actively considering you and inform them of your new job. Thank them graciously for their consideration. There are many other job seekers out there just like you who will benefit from having their candidacy improved when others bow out of the race. Who knows, you might at some future time have occasion to interact professionally with one of the organizations with which you sought employment. How embarrassing it would be to have someone remember you as the candidate who failed to notify them that you were taking a job elsewhere!

In all of your follow-up communications, keep good notes of whom you spoke with, when you called, and any instructions that were given about return communications. This will prevent any misunderstandings and provide you with good records of what has transpired.

Job Offer Considerations

For many recent college graduates, the thrill of their first job and, for some, the most substantial regular income they have ever earned seems an excess of good fortune coming at once. To question that first income or to be critical in any way of the conditions of employment at the time of the initial offer seems like looking a gift horse in the mouth. It doesn't seem to occur to many new hires even to attempt to negotiate any aspect of their first job. And, as many employers who deal with entry-level jobs for recent college graduates will readily confirm, the reality is that there simply isn't much movement in salary available to these new college recruits. The entry-level hire generally does not have an employment track record on a professional level to provide any leverage for negotiation. Real negotiations on salary, benefits, retirement provisions, and so forth come to those with significant employment records at higher income levels.

Of course, the job offer is more than just money. It can be composed of geographic assignment, duties and responsibilities, training, benefits, health and medical insurance, educational assistance, car allowance or company vehicle, and a host of other items. All of this is generally detailed in the formal letter that presents the final job offer. In most cases this is a follow-up to a personal phone call from the employer representative who has been principally responsible for your hiring process.

That initial telephone offer is certainly binding as a verbal agreement, but most firms follow up with a detailed letter outlining the most significant parts of your employment contract. You may, of course, choose to respond immediately at the time of the telephone offer (which would be considered a binding oral contract), but you will also be required to formally answer the letter of offer with a letter of acceptance, restating the salient elements of the employer's description of your position, salary, and benefits. This ensures that both parties are clear on the terms and conditions of employment and remuneration and any other outstanding aspects of the job offer.

Is This the Job You Want?

Most new employees will respond affirmatively in writing, glad to be in the position to accept employment. If you've worked hard to get the offer and the job market is tight, other offers may not be in sight, so you will say, "Yes, I accept!" What is important here is that the job offer you accept be one that does fit your particular needs, values, and interests as you've outlined them in your self-assessment process. Moreover, it should be a job that will not only use your skills and education but also challenge you to develop new skills and talents.

Jobs are sometimes accepted too hastily, for the wrong reasons, and without proper scrutiny by the applicant. For example, an individual might readily accept a sales job only to find the continual rejection by potential clients unendurable. An office worker might realize within weeks the constraints of a desk job and yearn for more activity. Employment is an important part of our lives. It is, for most of our adult lives, our most continuous productive activity. We want to make good choices based on the right criteria.

If you have a low tolerance for risk, a job based on commission will certainly be very anxiety-provoking. If being near your family is important, issues of relocation could present a decision crisis for you. If you're an adventurous person, a job with frequent travel would provide needed excitement and be very desirable. The importance of income, the need to continue your education, your personal health situation—all of these have an impact on whether the job you are considering will ultimately meet your needs. Unless you've spent some time understanding and thinking about these issues, it will be difficult to evaluate offers you do receive.

More important, if you make a decision that you cannot tolerate and feel you must leave that job, you will then have both unemployment and self-esteem issues to contend with. These will combine to make the next job search tough going, indeed. So make your acceptance a carefully considered decision.

Negotiate Your Offer

It may be that there is some aspect of your job offer that is not particularly attractive to you. Perhaps there is no relocation allotment to help you move your possessions, and this presents some financial hardship for you. It may be that the health insurance is less than you had hoped. Your initial assignment may be different from what you expected, either in its location or in the duties and responsibilities that comprise it. Or it may simply be that the salary is less than you anticipated. Other considerations may be your official starting date of employment, vacation time, evening hours, dates of training programs or schools, and other concerns.

If you are considering not accepting the job because of some item or items in the job offer "package" that do not meet your needs, you should know that most employers emphatically wish that you would bring that issue to their attention. It may be that the employer can alter it to make the offer more agreeable for you. In some cases it cannot be changed. In any event the employer would generally like to have the opportunity to try to remedy a difficulty rather than risk losing a good potential employee over an issue that might have been resolved. After all, they have spent time and funds in securing your services, and they certainly deserve an opportunity to resolve any possible differences.

Honesty is the best approach in discussing any objections or uneasiness you might have over the employer's offer. Having received your formal offer in writing, contact your employer representative and indicate your particular dissatisfaction in a straightforward manner. For example, you might ex-

plain that while you are very interested in being employed by this organization, the salary (or any other benefit) is less than you have determined you
require. State the terms you need, and listen to the response. You may be
asked to put this in writing, or you may be asked to hold off until the
firm can decide on a response. If you are dealing with a senior representative of the organization, one who has been involved in hiring for some time,
you may get an immediate response or a solid indication of possible
outcomes.

Perhaps the issue is one of relocation. Your initial assignment is in the
Midwest, and because you had indicated a strong West Coast preference, you
are surprised at the actual assignment. You might simply indicate that while
you understand the need for the company to assign you based on its needs,
you are disappointed and had hoped to be placed on the West Coast. You
could inquire if that were still possible and, if not, would it be reasonable
to expect a West Coast relocation in the future.

If your request is presented in a reasonable way, most employers will not
see this as jeopardizing your offer. If they can agree to your proposal, they
will. If not, they will simply tell you so, and you may choose to continue
your candidacy with them or remove yourself from consideration. The choice
will be up to you.

Some firms will adjust benefits within their parameters to meet the candidate's need if at all possible. If a candidate requires a relocation cost
allowance, he or she may be asked to forgo tuition benefits for the first year
to accomplish this adjustment. An increase in life insurance may be adjusted
by some other benefit trade-off; perhaps a family dental plan is not needed.
In these decisions you are called upon, sometimes under time pressure, to
know how you value these issues and how important each is to you.

Many employers find they are more comfortable negotiating for candidates who have unique qualifications or who bring especially needed expertise to the organization. Employers hiring large numbers of entry-level college
graduates may be far more reluctant to accommodate any changes in offer
conditions. They are well supplied with candidates with similar education
and experience so that if rejected by one candidate, they can draw new candidates from an ample labor pool.

Compare Offers

The condition of the economy, the job seeker's academic major and particular geographic job market, and individual needs and demands for certain
employment conditions may not provide more than one job offer at a time.
Some job seekers may feel that no reasonable offer should go unaccepted for
the simple fear there won't be another.

In a tough job market, or if the job you seek is not widely available, or when your job search goes on too long and becomes difficult to sustain financially and emotionally, it may be necessary to accept an inferior offer. The alternative is continued unemployment. Even here, when you feel you don't have a choice, you can at least understand that in accepting this particular offer, there may be limitations and conditions you don't appreciate. At the time of acceptance, there were no other alternatives, but you can begin to use that position to gain the experience and talent to move toward a more attractive position.

Sometimes, however, more than one offer is received, and the candidate has the luxury of choice. If the job seeker knows what he or she wants and has done the necessary self-assessment honestly and thoroughly, it may be clear that one of the offers conforms more closely to those expressed wants and needs.

However, if, as so often happens, the offers are similar in terms of conditions and salary, the question then becomes which organization might provide the necessary climate, opportunities, and advantages for your professional development and growth. This is the time when solid employer research and astute questioning during the interviews really pay off. How much did you learn about the employer through your own research and skillful questioning? When the interviewer asked during the interview "Do you have any questions?" did you ask the kinds of questions that would help resolve a choice between one organization and another? Just as an employer must decide among numerous applicants, so must the applicant learn to assess the potential employer. Both are partners in the job search.

Reneging on an Offer

An especially disturbing occurrence for employers and career counseling professionals is when a job seeker formally (either orally or by written contract) accepts employment with one organization and later reneges on the agreement and goes with another employer.

There are all kinds of rationalizations offered for this unethical behavior. None of them satisfies. The sad irony is that what the job seeker is willing to do to the employer—make a promise and then break it—he or she would be outraged to have done to him- or herself: have the job offer pulled. It is a very bad way to begin a career. It suggests the individual has not taken the time to do the necessary self-assessment and self-awareness exercises to think and judge critically. The new offer taken may, in fact, be no better or worse than the one refused. You should be aware that there have been incidents of legal action following job candidates' reneging on an offer. This adds a very sour note to what should be a harmonious beginning of a lifelong adventure.

PART TWO

THE CAREER PATHS

5

Introduction to the Psychology Career Paths

Do you remember using a special graphic feature in your anatomy textbook? It included a basic illustration of the human body and a series of transparent overlays for the venous system, the arterial system, the nervous system, and other important systems that make up the human anatomy. Laying one system on top of the other, you began to build a comprehensive picture of how the body works.

The anatomy of a career path in psychology can be described in much the same way. The outline of a career path is defined first with the broadest of brushstrokes. Think about workers overseeing congregate living in a residential setting; people in organizations managing human resources; teachers in the classroom educating students; and case managers working with clients to promote health and well-being in social and human services. Therapists use a variety of techniques to heal someone with a physical or mental illness through therapy.

There may be just a spark of intuitive interest in teaching or a preference for the humanistic outreach of social and community services. Some prefer the role-modeling and direct assistance opportunities afforded by group living, while others feel a deep need to assist individuals struggling with mental problems that might be alleviated through any number of interventions.

Read each of the five career paths and follow your instinct. That choice, which you may change many times, will become the basic illustration of your career anatomy. Thinking about some employment conditions (the overlays) will affect how you see your choice. You will have the outline of your original choice, but you'll gain a more complex, more complete understanding as you add layers of information and facts. Each successive overlay will refine and further define your career path through the choices you make about location, specialization, and your own needs and life goals.

The first overlay will be a template of your skills, interests, and abilities. You'll want to do a serious self-assessment like the one suggested at the opening of this book to think about the education requirements of each path. Does this career path make the best use of your skills and interests? For example, if you're a strong team builder and team player and enjoy working closely with many colleagues, therapy or social and human services provide more opportunities in that direction than residential care or even teaching.

The next important overlay might be that of the possible client populations: undergraduate or graduate students, individuals of different ages with mental illnesses or handicaps, seriously ill clients, or those having difficulty coping with life's stresses and strains. Each will make different demands on you. Which will you work with best and most effectively? Which population offers you the scope, growth, and, maybe, "stretch" we all need in an occupation?

Your third overlay has to do with the nature of the activity you want to primarily engage in. Teaching involves reading, research, lecturing, grading papers, and serving on committees. Therapy means intimate, sometimes physical, effort with clients to work toward healing. Residential care involves all the tasks in managing a home with the additional supervision and responsibility for your patient group. Social and human services work involves counseling, telephone work, significant paperwork, and lots of negotiation. Human resources requires listening skills as well as data-analysis, decision-making, and public-speaking abilities.

Other overlays are up to you. Financial reward may be important to you or even necessary if you are graduating with significant debt. Each of these jobs has a salary range, and some paths pay more than others. If your salary is critical or if you have specific income thresholds you must meet, then by all means, investigate possible salary differences for each path and add that overlay to your illustration.

Status, privacy or lack thereof, geographic location, supply and demand for jobs, promotion possibilities, and opportunities for professional growth are all individual concerns, and each constitutes another overlay as you build your composite picture of the best career path choice. You may choose to do this overlay exercise for each path that follows until you have a solid understanding of the pluses and minuses of each career choice.

Psychology as Education Rather than Training

The four-year degree is very often an entrance hurdle required to enter many segments of the job market today. Interestingly enough, aside from technical positions, most organizations are willing to and do train their entry-level college graduate employees for any number of management positions. The Japanese major becomes a university official, the geography major becomes a counselor, the English major is a salesperson, and the sociology major does telemarketing. The employer tends to see many liberal arts degrees as guarantees of "trainability" and not guarantees of subject area expertise. Some graduates end up in what they find, not in what they planned for.

Begin Planning Your Career

Liberal arts graduates often get sidetracked from their major when they enter the job market because they soon learn that their time in college was not job training. Unlike the business major, the education major, or the computer science graduate, the psychology major has been learning *about* psychology, not how to *do* psychology. And yet, as these paths demonstrate, if you prepare yourself and plan your career, many employers will be willing to take you on in jobs with a very direct use of your psychology background. You'll use every course you had and learn so much more.

The remaining chapters outline five career paths you can follow with your degree in psychology. These paths have been carefully selected to draw deeply on your psychology education. Many graduates who have liberal arts degrees say they don't need a four-year degree to do their work. The accounting major working in sales, the English major in retail, or the biology major in restaurant management all have the same lament: "What did I get my degree for?" But in reading the paths presented here, psychology majors will see that they can directly use what they learned in earning their degree.

The career paths explored are worth all the planning you can give them, because they depend upon and continue to build on the foundation of an excellent education in psychology. These career paths, and the many actual jobs illustrated for each, hold the promise of being able to enhance and enrich the time and effort you have spent in achieving your degree. Each can launch you on a career of unlimited possibilities, because they all involve human development and behavior.

What Paths Can You Take to Begin With?

The five career paths chosen for psychology are:

1. Residential care
2. Social and human services
3. Human resources
4. Therapy
5. Teaching

These paths are described in detail in Chapters 6 through 10, and each can help you create a complete set of overlays for specific careers that draw on your psychology background. They are offered as realistic and achievable suggestions, and they are presented to stimulate your thinking about possible directions as you enter the workforce. Each chapter is sprinkled with many actual job listings, so you can match your résumé or degree aspirations against what is being requested. Many travelers begin on the same road using the same basic career outline because entry-level jobs, even with different organizations, seem remarkably similar. Soon, however, the road diverges, and each person begins to acquire different skills and experiences in his or her life's work—creating unique overlays. It is the detail contained on each overly and the layering of them that will determine your career direction.

6

Path I: Residential Care

As a psychology major, you have come to understand a number of issues that affect American society. Human development and its stages and transitions are manifest in the familiar issues and concerns of American culture: body image, aging, midlife crisis, eating disorders, sexual orientation, depression, anxiety, and 1,001 other issues that influence our individual and collective mental health. The popularization of psychology, begun by an over-the-counter glossy magazine *Psychology Today* that was first published in 1968, was a visible manifestation of our concern with things psychological.

From your class work, reading, and professors you know enough to be suspicious of this attention. America is a great nation for fads, and psychology may be the beneficiary of that attention. We have seen a resurgence of the psychobiography, declared majors in undergraduate colleges, and an enormous increase in types of therapy and in individuals enrolling in such therapy. The number of psychotherapeutic drug prescriptions is on the increase, and particular drugs, such as Prozac, continue to be the subject of intense debate among physicians, psychologists, ethicists, and the person on the street.

Has anything changed? Are we more sensitive to mental health issues? Are our overall goals for health and well-being advancing? In the area of residential care, the answer must be a qualified *yes*. Increasing provision of residential care, the growing quality of residential care facilities, and the corresponding increase in professionalism and training of residential care staff and administration have created an awareness and an appreciation within the general public for the advantages and therapeutic rewards of noninstitutional care.

At an earlier and more naive time in our history of dealing with individuals who, either temporarily or permanently, varied from socially imposed norms, our solution was institutionalization. The social service, medical, legal, and humanitarian communities locked away everyone from psychotics to orphans. Hospitals, sanitariums, state hospitals (a well-known euphemism for mental institutions), homes (which, ironically, were closer to prisons), and prisons held people who were blind, mentally retarded or handicapped, epileptic, without speech, criminally insane, chronically depressed, or schizophrenic, as well as individuals with cerebral palsy, polio, multiple sclerosis, and cystic fibrosis.

No longer. Dramatic discoveries and improvements in drug therapy in areas such as schizophrenia and depression, the Community Mental Health Centers Act of 1963 (essentially eliminating mental hospitals), and increasing acceptance of people who are mentally and physically challenged in the workplace have spurred the creation of a variety of residential care options.

Even in the criminal justice system, the range of options in correctional institutions and prisons has expanded enormously. Day programs outside the institution, halfway houses that more closely resemble attractive rooming houses than prison facilities, and work-release programs all improve rehabilitation. They speed the reintroduction of the offender into society, reduce recidivism through retraining, and avoid the conditioning effects of incarceration. Ultimately, the cost to the tax-paying public is lowered.

Trying to define residential care is a challenge. You could be working as an overnight counselor in a small group home for delinquent adolescent boys. Or you could be a recreation therapist working nine to five in a luxury facility for older adults. Both are residential care positions, though the responsibilities, working conditions, and patient population are dramatically different.

To begin to define residential care, we can make the following general statements:

- Residents participate, to some degree, in their own care and maintenance (chores, shopping, group decisions, personal care).
- Both short-term and long-term living situations are available.
- There is an attempt to duplicate, insofar as possible, homelike conditions.
- Medical treatment is off-site.
- Generally, staff do not wear uniforms.
- A variety of therapies may be offered: general counseling, milieu therapy, recreational therapy, expressive therapies, and in some specific

situations (substance abuse recovery), drug and alcohol abuse treatments.

The Growing Importance of Residential Care

Several factors have played roles in the growing importance of residential care for a range of clients. First, the deinstitutionalization movement that began in the 1960s has resulted in a growing number of community-integrated homes and apartment-suite living situations for people with mental retardation or a mental handicap. Second, a host of other social issues is being addressed by government agencies, nonprofit organizations, and private, for-profit facilities, and residential care is a factor in their solutions. The various types of residential care facilities include group homes. These house people with various needs: recovering drug and substance abusers, young boys who are acting out different types of emotional and/or physical trauma, delinquents of both genders, and battered and abused women and children. The group home or psychiatric halfway house can accommodate any of the changing issues that society presents. Health-care professionals have found that clients do far better when they are brought together in a more homelike environment with caring role models than in the institutional settings of the past.

Besides making therapeutic sense, these residential care facilities make economic sense. One reason for lower costs is that these homes are based on group and individual therapy in a community milieu. Also, some clients can contribute more to their own care in a residential setting than they can in an institution. Maintenance, cooking, cleaning, and recreation can be self-managed in some group homes.

There is still much work to be done. A recent U.S. government General Accounting Office report on improving outcomes for youth leaving foster care demonstrated that, although forty states reported expanding independent living services to younger youth and thirty-six states expanded services to older youth, gaps remain in providing some key services, including residential services, to youth.

Definition of the Career Path

An oft-heard complaint of the newly minted psychology graduate is that all the jobs demand far more experience than the graduate has. You want to use your education and work in psychology, but where do you start?

The short answer to this very valid question is in residential care facilities, also known as psychiatric halfway houses, community residences for the mentally ill, group homes, shelters, and transitional living.

Kinds of Residential Care

Residential care can be defined using a number of discriminants. You can classify residential care by the average stay of clients, either short-term or long-term stays. You can define residential care by the amount of structure and/or therapeutic treatment that occurs in the residence. For instance, drug rehab care is very strict and ordered with many rigid routines and protocols to foster success and responsible behavior. Some residential care settings for employed individuals with mental handicaps are not very different from group apartment living. Others legitimately want to categorize residential care by the population served (presenting issues): the aged, adolescent delinquents, recovering drug abusers, battered women, or pregnant teenage girls. Each of these categorizations has implications for you and your employment suitability.

Duration of Residence. How long your clients stay at the residential care facility may be important to you because it affects your interaction with clients. At one end of the spectrum, in short-term residences, you may have a constantly changing population of clients and little time to effect much change. You can provide comfort, counseling, sustenance, security, and many basic needs. There may be time for some referrals but generally not for long-term follow-up. The pace may be rapid with much diversity, and there may be little closure. On the other hand, long-term facilities allow you to work intensively with clients and mark progress over time. Therapeutic options for connection with your clients increase with duration of residence. There can be, as well, a corresponding static quality, with little dramatic change day to day.

Structure. How involved you want to be in working with your clients will have something to do with the appeal of different types of residential care structures. Each residential care facility has its own mission and goals. Some simply provide clean, comfortable living arrangements for clients who are functioning well and who may even be working but need to return to a secure, stable environment. These clients may have trouble with stress or too many challenges but essentially want as much autonomy as they can reasonably handle. Your role is to provide what is needed.

At the opposite end of the spectrum are facilities in which you may have to physically restrain clients from time to time, partner them in personal-care activities, provide recreational and maintenance activities, and supervise and monitor behavior rather closely.

Presenting Issues. The presenting issues that bring clients together in a residential unit may be more important to you than how long a client stays at your facility or how intrusive you are in your client's daily life. You may have a deep interest in the ability of people with Down's syndrome to integrate into society. Or you may feel a strong pull to work with children who have been sexually or physically abused. A disease, a social problem, or a mental health challenge may draw you to a client population to begin your career in residential care.

Residential Care: A Demand for Qualified Staff

Residential care creates an enormous demand for staff. When you take the previously large capacity of medical and psychiatric facilities and break those living units down into smaller, house-sized communities, you can understand how the need for staff multiplies. In addition, most of these homes require what is called "awake overnight counselors" to be available to clients during the night and to monitor house activity. Day staffers can be involved in patient treatment plans, job counseling, and teaching a variety of daily skills and personal-care standards. It is challenging, demanding, and physically tiring work. It draws on staff members' ingenuity, patience, strength, and emotional reserves.

A Place to Begin Your Career

Turnover in residential care is high, and that needs to be understood up front. Residential care is not career employment. Turnover is above normal because the job is demanding, generally salaries are not competitive, and there are many, many challenges. Professionals who hire for residential staff positions often prefer hiring the candidate who is "on the way" to something else. Many jobs are labeled "entry level," and the job announcement indicates that training and/or mentoring will be provided. A recent, typical job announcement said:

Youth Counselor. Entry-level position in a secure, clinically intensive residential treatment program. Seeking enthusiastic and motivated individual to work as part of a team of professionals. Use your psychology degree to be a pivotal person in a youth's life. Provide counseling in the areas of social skills and job, school, and community preparedness. Gain hands-on, practical experience that allows for professional growth in the counseling field. Increase and develop your skills in the area of counseling through learning crisis counseling and clinical skills. Also learn to facilitate and run therapeutic groups. Excellent training and professional development available. No previous experience necessary; we're happy to train the right person.

The Challenging Reality of Residential Care

Most residential care jobs are advertised as "counselor" positions, and that job title may attract you. Several entry-level positions that a psychology bachelor's degree recipient with an internship and part-time work experience would be eligible to apply for follow.

• **Residential counselor.** Maintain and track resident files and progress, conduct therapeutic programs, develop relationships with caseworkers for current and potential residents. Degree required.

• **Residential clinician—overnight.** Four-year degree and one year of experience required. Competent, caring person with solid clinical skills. Facility serves consumers diagnosed with mental illness and drug and alcohol dependency.

• **Residential counselor.** Head injury program looking for residential counselors interested in doing work that makes a difference. Help individuals live safely, maintain their physical and emotional health, foster relationships with housemates, and develop skills necessary to increase individuals' independence. Bachelor's degree required.

• **Residential mental health worker.** Provide excellent care and treatment services for severely emotionally disturbed children. Willingness to learn agency-approved therapeutic crisis intervention techniques required. Four-year degree and some experience required.

• **Residential counselor.** Join interdisciplinary clinical team to work with adolescents at private residential treatment facility. Serve as role model for socially effective values, attitudes, and behaviors. Ensure activities are conducted in safe and positive environment. Occasionally escort residents outside of facility. Requires undergraduate degree in psychology, sociology, or related field.

• **Residential counselor.** Direct care and supervision of youths in residential setting. B.A./B.S. in human services field required. Graveyard shifts available with 10 percent paid differential above starting base salary.

This list begins to highlight the range of duties required of residential care workers:

- Caring about the clients
- Creating a therapeutic atmosphere
- Counseling
- Assisting with daily living skills
- Assisting with skill development
- Effecting transitions
- Integrating residents

Although many duties involve case management, other duties are also required, including:

- Responding to emergencies
- Handling public relations activities
- Supervising staff members
- Carrying out administrative duties

What's important in assessing these residential care positions is (1) your understanding of the duties and responsibilities and (2) your readiness to undertake this work. This is important work, and it's critical that interested, qualified, and skilled people be in these positions.

Caring About the Clients

The work is challenging. These jobs require the residential care worker to have endless resources of patience and a caring, thoughtful attitude. Residents will present a variety of behaviors and abilities to manage independent living, and the residential care worker will continually be required to draw on deep reserves of understanding and tact to help the clients become more adept at group living, interpersonal skills, and general life skills.

Creating a Therapeutic Atmosphere

Residential counselors and other staff members are responsible for creating the proper therapeutic atmosphere to facilitate the growth and nurturance of residents. They are often responsible for the selection of new residents. They create house policy, educate residents on its implementation, and carry through the policies. How these duties are undertaken affects the atmosphere of the facility.

Counseling

Counseling is a process of connection and deep human involvement between people. There are many formal schools of counseling theory and technique, but individual counselors ultimately evolve a counseling technique that works for them and their clients. For the clientele of the residential care worker, the deeply empathic listening attention of the counselor is often in and of itself therapeutic. Clients who have a caring listener who values them as individuals and to whom they can talk about their problems are able to begin their journey back to healthy living.

Assisting with Daily Living Skills

Residential care came about in large part because the inability of many clients to self-manage daily living tasks was recognized. They can do quite a lot, and those who can master daily living skills find increased self-esteem and pride in their efforts. Most often in long-term residential settings, there may be some clients who are unable to carry out the basic daily care functions: feeding themselves, getting dressed, bathing, brushing their teeth, or taking care of their elimination requirements. Paraprofessionals often handle these activities, but you must be prepared to assist residents as needed, striking a delicate balance between actual assistance and teaching.

Assisting with Skill Development

Residential care workers assist residents with all sorts of skill development, from the art of negotiating turf issues, recreational choices, and music volume with their fellow residents, to practical skills in cooking, crisis management, and medication administration. Assistance with educational plans also may be involved.

Effecting Transitions

When residents leave to return home or to move on to independent housing arrangements, the residential care counselor has often helped to secure those new housing arrangements, acting as an intermediary with new landlords, neighbors, or the family to ensure an easy and stress-free transition for the resident.

Integrating Residents

Residential care professionals also play a role in community education. It would hardly be helpful to neighbors, children, and the general public to be unaware of the inhabitants of residential care facilities. Sitting on bright summer furniture and planting colorful bedding flowers may be enough activity for an elderly population that is not entirely mobile, but caring for other groups of clients, especially the mentally challenged, can involve far more activity.

Regular trips to shopping malls, the grocery store, pizza parties, or birthdays at the local McDonald's help the general public, in a low-risk, non-threatening way, begin to understand and appreciate these people as part of their community. These same residents could effect no better demonstration of their similarities to their neighbors than being out on the lawn on a crisp fall day raking leaves! Some things are the same for all of us.

Responding to Emergencies

Residential care workers need to be ready to respond to emergencies as varied as power outages or resident conflicts. They may be required to obtain or administer medical assistance for residents, which demands not only excellent record keeping but maintaining a clear, cool head in an emergency. Many emergencies are no different from our own home crises: frozen water pipes, power failures, a personal injury. However, depending on the client population, some of these can be frightening at worst or overstimulating at the very least. Residential care professionals need to be able to anticipate problems and be prepared to respond

Handling Public Relations Activities

In addition to managing the residence, residential care professionals also serve as public relations officers and spokespersons for the residence to community groups, newspaper reporters, telephone callers, and neighborhood groups. This in itself can be a challenge because the psychiatric or community residence home can have difficulty being accepted in some areas.

Understanding and appreciating the public's objections and concerns is an essential step in beginning to respond to those concerns. Educating the public about the mission of your facility, profiling the residents as individuals, and not labeling them as a group are critical. By being out in the community and stressing residents' contributions at their jobs or through their volunteer work, or by explaining the economics of residential care, versus costly institutionalized care, you can help the public understand the value of these residences.

Supervising Staff Members

Some residential care workers are responsible for handling matters relating to staffing. They schedule the work rotations of ancillary staff and are principally responsible for the hiring, training, and evaluation. As with any management position, clear and consistent communication is important and that is magnified with twenty-four-hour shifts. Well-maintained duty rosters, detailed job specifications, frequent feedback, and staff meetings create an esprit de corps that staff members respond to.

Carrying Out Administrative Duties

House managers may collect rent and maintain accounting records for all residents. They also oversee the operating budget for food, house maintenance, and furnishings, and they will often supervise any outside contract workers conducting maintenance such as heavy cleaning.

Not every residential care position brings all of these requirements with it. Each job will have its own unique combination of responsibilities and areas of emphasis. However, no matter what their primary duties, some professionals have said that during the course of twelve months, they touch on each and every one of the elements just listed.

As a result, the psychology major looking for entry-level employment who wants a position that will not only challenge him or her to develop new skills but use existing talents in a new environment will find residential care worthy of the job search.

Use Your Residential Counseling Position to Grow

What most typically happens in this career path is that after you have worked in the residential care setting, you will want to become more involved therapeutically in the care plans for these clients. To be able to do so will involve returning to school for additional course work, training, and/or degrees. During this process, you will return to your experiences from your residential care position again and again.

Leaving residential care for a new position in the helping professions, you will discover you are well situated for a number of openings in social and community service, therapy, administration and management, and counseling. Much depends on the particular emphasis in your residential experience and the particular role you played. Subsequent chapters outline career paths for which residential care would provide an excellent jumping-off point.

As you progress in your residential care job, your responsibility is to ensure that you are building a portfolio of success that will allow you flexibility. Are you keeping samples of evaluation materials you designed for your staff? Have you typed up notes from your in-service training presentations and compiled samples of programs you could present? If you've been successful in placing newspaper articles about residents and the home, have you collected those? A personal journal or process notes on your therapeutic interactions will reinforce your memory and allow you to illustrate interview questions with anonymous but specific anecdotes about successful client interactions. Collect letters of recommendation from the many professionals in multiple disciplines you work with on behalf of your clients. All of these efforts will help you present your story to a new employer as you move forward on your career path.

Working Conditions

Working conditions in residential care are interesting, to say the least. Do you remember, as a college student, going home for the weekend and trying to get that big paper written? Or perhaps you had your own apartment at college. The telephone, the television, the refrigerator, the CD player all proved to be hard-to-resist distractions. Sometimes, even taking the trash out or doing laundry was preferable to writing that paper. You'll face similar issues and distractions in residential care.

Privacy

Living in and working at your job in a residential care facility will cause you to think about how much privacy you need. It's your home (at least for many hours a week) and your place of work. Some residential care managers have a separate apartment on the premises, but it can easily become everyone's space. And if your facility operates twenty-four hours a day, there are the comings and goings of each shift of care workers. It can be a challenge to carve out time for yourself or to separate your personal life from your work life.

Hands On

Residential care is interactive care. Besides the possibilities that exist for actually assisting some of your clients in basic personal-care skills, this is not a good job for someone who wants to stand off in the distance and supervise or sit down and just talk. There is hands-on home maintenance to execute and organize, dishes to be done, meals to prepare, spills to mop up, and bathrooms to clean—all the normal duties of running a house. Certainly, in most cases your residents will play the dominant role in these chores, but you need to be ready to pitch in and show how it's done or lend a hand when things need to be done faster.

Teamwork

In most cases, your clients will be receiving other kinds of help, which, depending on their situation, could range from drug therapy to rehabilitative services. You are part of a care team, and you will probably meet with many of these caregivers as you work with your individual residents. You will share your clients' progress, behaviors, and needs to ensure the team is functioning in the best interest of the clients.

Staffing in the residence itself is apt to be lean, although your facility may be staffed around the clock. During some periods during the day, you might even be alone while residents are out working, shopping, doing volunteer work, or receiving therapy. You will need to have an outlet for your social instincts during your free time if your work unit is small or if you are by yourself.

Training and Qualifications

Your motivation for seeking a residential care job and your background are very important considerations as you make your decision. Think about both carefully.

Your Motives Must Be Healthy

Attitudinally, residential care workers must display the proper motivation for residential care work. The motivation is not to "rescue" or enable residents to feel dependent upon you. Instead, it requires a professional detachment that will foster the focus required to perform needs analysis and to create effective solutions that empower and strengthen each resident.

Expect Extensive Screening

Administrators charged with hiring residential care workers are primarily concerned that the candidates present healthy and appropriate psychiatric profiles, so they may request a psychiatric assessment by a consultant. Motivation, stability, and intentionality of the house leadership are all critical to the success of the residential care program, so applicants are screened carefully and references assiduously verified. Prior academic and job performance are reviewed, as they tend to reflect future performance.

Earnings

Information on salaries for residential care positions is available if you look in the right places. To gain the best insight and most up-to-date figures, review job postings on a website such as CareerBuilder (careerbuilder.com), where many of the positions list a salary. Or, review the Occupational Employment Statistics (available online at bls.gov and at many libraries) and review the section on Counselors, All Other. Salary data relating to two industries—individual and family services and residential mental health facilities—accurately reflect current salaries for residential care counselors.

Entry-level salaries will vary by type of employer. Some of the highest salaries come from corporate residential care facilities. Independent social service agencies, church-affiliated outreach programs, or municipal programs may pay far less for the same work demands. While salary ranges given here are expressed as yearly amounts, in most cases you will find pay expressed as an hourly rate. At the time this book was published, entry-level salaries for residential (nonsupervisory) positions ranged from about $21,630 to $26,350. Supervisory positions for those with bachelor's degrees who have approximately two years' experience in administration and/or supervision were $27,500 to $36,000.

Because entry-level salaries are modest, it's even more important that you develop a realistic budget as suggested during the self-assessment in Chapter 1. With a new job, and a demanding and potentially stressful one at that, it's important that it meet at least your minimum salary needs. As with any first job, although the salary may be more than you've ever made, you'll want to be sure it can cover your basic needs, including food, shelter, and transportation. You may be surprised at the sum total of your anticipated expenses, especially if a car loan or school financial aid payback expense is involved.

Do a thorough expense analysis, and you can be more specific with an employer about your minimum salary requirements. In accepting any job it is your responsibility—not the employer's—to be sure that the salary offered will allow you to support yourself. You would be very distressed to find you had underestimated your expenses and had to leave a new position because of lack of funds. Your short tenure in the position and reason for leaving could adversely affect your ability to secure new employment.

In positions where you are able to meet your minimum salary need, but the pay is still lower than you'd hoped for, don't overlook the value of the benefits package that may be provided. Many job postings indicate that excellent benefits are available. One benefit that you may be especially interested in is tuition reimbursement. Remember, this residential care job begins your career, and you may be able to acquire some additional education you'll need to move on in your career path. The following are two typical job advertisements outlining benefits provided.

Gender Responsive Therapist. Preferred candidate will possess a bachelor's degree in psychology or related field. Candidates with experience working with girls in residential and/or community settings a plus. We offer competitive wages, health and dental insurance, tuition assistance, and a 401(k) plan.

Residence Manager. Needed for community residence serving people with developmental disabilities. Bachelor's degree in related field required. We offer competitive salaries and medical and dental coverage, tuition assistance, generous time-off policy, and an agency-funded pension plan.

Career Outlook

The outlook for residential care positions is excellent. According to the U.S. Department of Labor, Bureau of Labor Statistics (bls.gov), the number of residential care positions is expected to grow dramatically through 2012. In fact, residential care positions (under the general classification of social and human service assistants) are listed among the six fastest growing occupations for the decade. The number of available positions is expected to increase 48 percent by 2012.

The outlook is positive for a number of reasons. First, with the success of treatment for a variety of mental and emotional disorders in the home-like settings of residences, there is increasing appreciation and demand for this kind of treatment setting. Second, the residential care option is more cost effective. Finally, numerous job openings will occur as current residential care workers retire or leave the profession.

A Growing Appreciation for Residential Care

Although the objection to individual home establishments has not lessened in some communities, the number of residences continues to grow. As their acceptance increases and the notoriety of their presence fades, an increasing public acceptance and appreciation for their mission and work should follow.

Reducing Costs

A strong rationale for residential care is economic. Opinion is quite clear that these populations do not belong in hospitals or large mental health institutions, and they do far better in the secure and homelike milieu created by the group residence. Behavior improves, medication demands lessen, and patients add to their repertoire of coping skills and behaviors. Residential care costs are easier to maintain and monitor and are appreciably lower than larger institutions with higher overhead.

Turnover in Employment

As stated previously, residential care is a starting point for a career, so there is a natural turnover as young workers gain experience and then move on to other professions that pay higher wages and value the direct experience gained in this field.

Strategy for Finding the Jobs

Your strategy for obtaining employment in residential care should include several tactics: taking relevant nonpsychology course work, exploring and choosing a setting in which you would most like to work, gaining supervisory experience, promoting your degree in psychology, and making clear your aspirations for career growth beyond residential care. Before you are ready to begin this work, however, be sure to revisit the self-assessment you completed. It will be useful as you begin your job search. Residential care is deeply rewarding but makes commensurate demands on many personal attributes, including your energy, patience, cooperation, and decision-making abilities.

Take Relevant Nonpsychology Course Work

If you are still in school, you may want to use your elective credits or the option of a minor to build an area of specialization that enhances your credentials. If you have graduated, continuing education courses allow you the same opportunities. Skills and abilities that will interest potential employers may be in any of several fields, including leisure or recreation, business, or communications.

Skills in leisure time use or recreation are important because residential workers often lead these types of activities. Facilities may offer arts and crafts, music, and recreation classes to provide a full leisure-time menu for residents so necessary to the therapeutic atmosphere of group living.

Some basic business courses that enhance the credentials you bring to the workplace include personnel and staffing, marketing, financial management, public relations, and business communications. Consider whether you are interested in building a knowledge base in this area.

Good communications skills are essential in working with residents, ancillary care workers, and volunteers and in carrying out public communications with interested community groups. Courses may be offered in communications, English, or business degree programs. No matter where you decide to work, these communications skills will only enhance what you have to offer.

Choose a Residential Care Setting

As you have read, the residential care path has a wide range of work sites from which to choose. You may feel a little overwhelmed by the number of possibilities. Which would be best for you? Think back to your reactions as you read about different situations. You could probably picture yourself in some work environments. You may have been particularly interested in the presenting issues that are addressed in a particular residential care environment (e.g., learning disabilities, mental retardation, or child abuse). Begin your job search by exploring a couple of the types of work settings whose client concerns will engage you.

You'll also want to talk with people working in the field. Use your college or university career network to identify a group of contacts or talk with professionals working at facilities in the geographic area where you live. In your conversations, ask people to explain in detail what their particular setting is like. What are the client demands? What kinds of presenting problems are evident and what are the particular challenges posed by these clients? Is it a quiet, clean, and neat setting? Is it a noisy and busy setting? Are necessary supplies easily obtained or are there ongoing funding issues? How often does the schedule rotation change? Begin to determine how this information meshes with what you learned about yourself in the self-assessment you undertook as a beginning step in the job-search process. You'll see that there are some settings that "fit" better with who you are and what you want in a job. Begin your job search with opportunities in those settings.

Try to Gain Some Level of Supervisory Experience

Because staff turnover in residential settings is high, moves from a staff care-taker position to a supervisory position can take place fairly quickly. Regardless of the specific setting, those with previous supervisory experience will be considered first for these positions. If, for example, you have experience in the food-service industry and you were able to move from a wait staff position into a managerial position, as you write your résumé and as you talk with potential employers in an interview emphasize your ability to take on increasing responsibilities. We have already described course work you may want to consider that will enhance your ability to supervise or manage a residential care facility.

Promote Your Degree in Psychology

As you studied psychology, you built a strong foundation that will allow you to carry out the "helping" duties that are required in residential care and the many more administrative duties that are also required. You'll have the ability to communicate effectively with other staff and multidisciplinary team members. You'll be able to handle public relations activities by writing clear and concise statements for the public and responding to verbal questions in an appropriate way. Your analytical skills can be used to quickly develop an appropriate response to an emergency. Add to this list and be ready to express all your talents as you write or refine your résumé and talk with potential employers.

Express Your Hopes for Growth

Often, potential employers will appreciate that someone seeking a residential care position is simply beginning a career in and is interested in increased responsibility, possibly in the form of residential care management. Those job candidates who are forthright and honest about expectations for career growth may be perceived as having the best disposition for this kind of demanding role.

Residential care is an opening to much larger vistas of work as a helping professional. It is demanding and draining, and it is expected that you will want to move on, enriched and strengthened in your career choice by this beginning.

Possible Employers

We've defined residential care according to three discriminates: duration of residence, structure, and presenting issues. Here we present a range of possible employers that highlights these factors.

Retirement Communities

Retirement communities represent a wide range of options for aging adults who no longer want to, or who cannot, maintain a household of their own. Some communities serve frail clients who can undertake very few efforts on their own and who require a great deal of assistance. In this setting, residential care workers would be responsible primarily for meeting the physical needs of their clients: feeding, bathing, dressing, or moving within the facility. Other retirement communities present more of a social setting, and the residential care worker would be more likely to focus on providing leisure activities for residents.

Help in Locating These Employers. Two career guides that provide useful information on career paths that involve working with senior citizens are *Opportunities in Gerontology and Aging Services Careers* and *The Helping Professions: A Careers Sourcebook.* In addition, use the yellow pages (online or print version) to locate facilities within a given geographic area. Look under headings such as Retirement and Life-Care Communities and Homes. Organizations that will be able to assist you in locating facilities include local social and human services agencies that serve elderly persons, or contact the American Association of Homes and Services for the Aging in Washington, D.C. (aahsa.org).

Community Mental Health Providers

Community mental health residential facilities can serve clients of every age and means. While some communities directly operate residential facilities for people who are dealing with issues related to mental and emotional health, others contract with for-profit or not-for-profit agencies to handle this need.

Help in Locating These Employers. A thorough review of related chapters in the VGM Career Books' *Careers in Social and Rehabilitation Services* will prove to be invaluable in explaining the complicated mental health system. This book also contains professional associations and professional and trade periodicals. The Substance Abuse and Mental Health Services Administration (SAMHSA) and its Center for Mental Health Services (CMHS) have a National Health Information Center website (mentalhealth.org). By navigating to Resources and then Mental Health Services Locator, you will find a list of directories and locators showing, state-by-state, many potential employment sites. You can then use a search engine to locate the specific residential care community mental health programs that are listed and review their job postings.

State Mental Health Providers
Every state provides support to its residents for handling issues related to mental health. Different states call their agencies by different names, but some of the more common ones include:

- Department of Mental Health and Mental Retardation
- Department of Health and Social Services
- Department of Health Services
- Department of Human Services
- Department of Mental Health
- Department of Institutions
- Department of Health and Rehabilitative Services

These agencies offer a variety of services, some of which the state directly provides, while other services are contracted out to both for-profit and not-for-profit agencies.

Help in Locating These Employers. Your telephone directory lists state mental health agencies, or you can use a resource such as the Internet's Health Guide USA: America's Online Health Resource Guide (http://health guideusa.org/state_mental_health_agencies.htm), which lists all state mental health agencies. No two state sites are organized the same way, but each provides information about the state's mental health agency and will link you with state job announcements.

Substance Abuse Treatment Programs
Whether it relates to drugs or alcohol, substance abuse cuts across all age, ethnic, and social groups. Many residential workers specializing in substance abuse work at halfway houses for recovering alcoholics. Emerging data show that treatment programs should differ given the age and gender of the client, so some treatment facilities may focus on a specific population. These programs may be funded by the state, community, or private organizations or by some combination of these.

Help in Locating These Employers. The *Medical and Health Information Directory* contains three volumes, the third of which lists clinics, treatment centers, care programs, and counseling/diagnostic services for many subject areas. These directories are expensive, so your best bet to find them is a larger library. Because the field is changing and often underfunded, the Internet remains a more up-to-date source of information. One good site is the National Association of Addiction Treatment Providers (naatp.org). Members can be listed by state and there are links to the treatment providers' websites. Or use a search engine and enter "addiction treatment." You'll find leads to guides and directories, associations and support, clinics and treatment, and many related categories by addiction type. It's an excellent beginning resource.

Short-Term Youth Shelters

There are short-term residential programs for abused, acting-out boys or girls; runaway children; troubled children and youth ages seven through eighteen; substance-abusing youth; and youth involved in the criminal justice system. If you are interested in working with young people, this type of residential facility is worth investigating.

Help in Locating These Employers. When we entered "short-term youth shelters" in a search engine, we found a link to the YMCA Project Safe Place. This program provides access to immediate help and supportive resources for young people in crisis through a network of sites sustained by qualified agencies, trained volunteers, and businesses. If you navigate to the Links option (safeplaceservices.org/links.html), you can access lists of short-term youth shelters in the various regions of the United States. Some of the listings link you directly to that shelter's website where job openings are shown. And as with state and community mental health services, you'll want to network to discover the range of sites available in your area. Don't forget to scan your local yellow pages (online or print version) under a category such as Social and Human Services. An excellent choice on the Web is the U.S. Government, Department of Health and Human Services, Administration for Children and Families home page at acf.dhhs.gov.

Schools for Students with Special Education Needs

Many schools that offer residential programs serve students who have special education needs. Because these students live at the school, staff is needed outside of class hours to oversee student activities. Residential care workers help students pursue their studies. They take students on field trips, oversee students' leisure and living activities, and provide a safe and secure environment.

Help in Locating These Employers. Three resources that will help you locate residential programs that serve students with learning disabilities include *The Handbook of Private Schools* (available in libraries), *American Boarding Schools*, and Peterson's website, petersons.com/pschools, where you can find a comprehensive listing of independent secondary schools that offer programs and promote assistance to students with learning disabilities.

Possible Job Titles

You will see a range of job titles as you conduct your search for these kinds of positions. The title reflects the level of supervisory capability the job requires. Review the following list and add to it as you identify sites where you are interested in working.

Activities coordinator
Assistant manager
Case manager
Caseworker
Child-care worker
Counselor
Crisis worker
House manager
House parent
Mental health worker
Program assistant
Program manager
Psychiatric residence staffer
Relief worker
Residential clinician
Residential counselor
Residential specialist
Residential worker
Resident services provider
Special school counselor

Support worker
Youth-service worker

A growing movement considers the worker with a baccalaureate degree to be a professional. In the five career paths chosen for this book, that is emphatically so. But be aware that the term *paraprofessional* is also used to indicate someone in the mental health field who has not had formal educational training beyond high school, so carefully review the required qualifications for each job listing you examine. Avoid jobs that would underemploy you or that wouldn't allow you to use your full range of knowledge and skills.

Related Occupations

Residential care workers use many skills that have been developed in academic programs in psychology and in various work settings. These counseling, integrating, and supervising skills can also be put to use in many other types of work. Consider the following list and explore related occupations described in this book as well as in other resources you've found useful in your job search.

Career counselor
College student-affairs professional
Job developer
Labor relations specialist
Mental health counselor
Occupational therapist
Physical therapist
Social worker
Youth corrections officer

This list is just a teaser of the many related job titles that could be included here. Be sure to add to it as you study career possibilities that can use your psychology degree.

Professional Associations

Many organizations that serve clients who may need residential care are listed below. Be sure to review each listing and decide whether the association offers services that may be useful in your job search.

American Association of Homes and Services for the Aging
2519 Connecticut Ave. NW
Washington, DC 20008
aahsa.org
Members/Purpose: Voluntary nonprofit and governmental homes, housing, and health-related facilities and services for the elderly; state associations; interested individuals
Training: Provides educational program
Journals/Publications: *AAHSA Directory of Members*
Job Listings: aahsa.org/careers/job_mart/available.asp

American Mental Health Counselors Association
801 N. Fairfax St., Suite 304
Alexandria, VA 22314
amhca.org
Members/Purpose: Enhances the profession of mental health counseling through licensing, advocacy, education, and professional development
Journals/Publications: *Journal of Mental Health Counseling*; *Behavioral Healthcare Tomorrow*
Job Listings: Jobs listed on website

**Association of Halfway House Alcoholism Programs
of North America**
860 N. Center St.
Mesa, Arizona 85201
ahhap.org
Members/Purpose: Halfway house corporations, staff, board members, and individuals closely related to the halfway house movement
Training: Offers workshops and conferences
Journals/Publications: Online AHHAP membership directory (with links to some member websites); communications and services newsletter; conference proceedings

Canadian Counselling Association
16 Concourse Gate, Suite 600
Ottawa, ON K2E 7S8
Canada
ccacc.ca
Members/Purpose: Dedicated to the enhancement of the counseling profession in Canada
Training: Worldwide conferences listed on website

Journals/Publications: *Canadian Journal of Counselling*; *Cognica* (quarterly newsletter)
Job Listings: Jobs listed on website

Child Welfare League of America
440 1st St. NW, Third Floor
Washington, DC 20001
cwla.org
Members/Purpose: Privately and publicly supported membership organization devoted to the improvement of care and services for deprived, dependent, or neglected children, youth, and their families
Journals/Publications: *Child Welfare Journal*; *Children's Voice*; *Children's Monitor*; *Get Connected!* newsletter; CWLA directory of member agencies

Learning Disabilities Association of America
4156 Library Rd.
Pittsburgh, PA 15234
ldanatl.org
Members/Purpose: Parents of children with learning disabilities; interested professionals
Journals/Publications: LDA newsbriefs; *Learning Disabilities: A Multidisciplinary Journal*; *When Pre-Schoolers Are Not "On-Target"*

National Adult Day Services Association, Inc.
2519 Connecticut Ave. NW
Washington, DC 20008
nadsa.org
Members/Purpose: Committed to providing its members with effective national advocacy, educational and networking opportunities, research and communication
Training: Annual meeting is part of the American Association of Homes and Services for the Aging Annual Meeting and Exposition
Job Listings: Jobs listed on website

National Association for Children's Behavioral Health
1025 Connecticut Ave. NW, Suite 1012
Washington, DC 20036
nacbh.org

Members/Purpose: Promote the availability and delivery of appropriate and relevant services to children and youth with, or at risk of, serious emotional or behavioral disturbances and their families

Training: Convenes educational meetings twice a year

Journals/Publications: Online directory of members organized by state

National Association of Addiction Treatment Providers

313 W. Liberty St., Suite 129

Lancaster, PA 17603-2748

naatp.org

Members/Purpose: Corporate and private institutional alcohol and/or drug dependency treatment facilities that promote, assist, and enhance the delivery of ethical, effective, research-based treatment for alcoholism and other drug addictions

Training: Conducts seminars on marketing, management, and reimbursement

Journals/Publications: NAATP monthly newsletters; updated salary survey

Job Listings: Jobs listed on website

National Council for Community Behavioral Healthcare

12300 Twinbrook Pkwy., Suite 320

Rockville, MD 20852

nccbh.org

Members/Purpose: Represents the providers of mental health, substance abuse, and developmental disability services. Members serve more than 4.5 million adults, children, and families each year and employ more than 250,000 staff

Training: Offers annual training conference

Journals/Publications: National Council News monthly newsletter

Job Listings: Members can access job listings on the website and in the newsletter.

National Network for Youth

1319 F St. NW, Suite 401

Washington, DC 20004

nn4youth.org

Members/Purpose: Provides education, networking, training, materials, and policy work with federal, state, and local lawmakers. Members include community-based organizations as well as youth, adults, associations, and regional and state networks of youth workers that provide street-based services, emergency shelter, transitional living programs, counseling, and social, health, educational, and job-related services to more than 2.5 million youth annually.

Training: Offers annual symposium and targeted professional development opportunities

Journals/Publications: At a Glance e-newsletter; *Network News* quarterly newsletter

Job Listings: Job opportunities listed on website

7

Path 2: Social and Human Services

Stop reading this book right now! Put it down and go visit a website such as socialservice.com, or look up Social and Human Services in the yellow pages (online or print version). No matter which source you use, a significant number of agencies will be listed. Many you'll recognize immediately, such as the American Red Cross, your state legal assistance fund, the American Heart Association, or local and state family planning groups. But other unfamiliar agency names might be interesting, for example, your state's assistive technology and equipment center or a program of academic excellence. Other organizations focus on issues such as helping people with AIDS or housing difficulties or fuel assistance. Some programs offer abortion counseling or counseling for young people or help for people with disabilities. Investigate them all.

Helping: A Pervasive Need

As you explore social and human services websites or look through the yellow pages for a large metropolitan area, a staggering number of social services organizations will be listed. Not only will you probably be surprised at how narrowly focused some of the agency programs are, but you may also be surprised at the number of organizations listed under a particular heading. So, while you may be very interested to know there are workers concentrating on housing assistance issues, you may be even more surprised to see so many organizations listed under that heading.

These listings serve as symbols of both our social concerns and our social consciousness. They are clear signs of what is wrong in our society in the needs they express and also what is right in our society since there is an agency to help. It's fair to say that the size of these listings has as much to do with the size of the community as with the concern the community expresses for others and the determination of those committed to the public good to operate organizations and agencies to help.

So Many Receive Social and Human Services

The choice of populations and clients to work with is wide, indeed. Each group presents its own set of issues and makes demands on and challenges the social and human services worker. Here's a selected list of some of the most prominent populations with a capsule description of relevant issues and statistics.

Aging

The need for social and human services generally increases with age, and the elderly population is one of the fastest growing in this country. In a Web publication titled U.S. Growing Bigger, Older, and More Diverse, the Population Reference Bureau (prb.org) states that we are "on the brink of an elderly boom." The aging of the baby boomers is driving this change, which in 2030 will result in one in five people claiming an age of sixty-five or older, compared to one in eight in 2005. The fastest growing segment of this population is people age eighty-five or older. It is projected that in 2010, six million people will be in this age bracket, and by 2050 there will be twenty-one million.

Even though some seniors may be more physically active or financially protected than their predecessors, there is still an increased need for physical therapy, transportation services, counseling for depression and emotional difficulties, and help coping with changes, including living circumstances and diet. Although some elderly individuals can afford to reside in planned communities, others live alone or in a variety of other settings. Some are in hospitals, nursing homes, or facilities that care for people with mental illnesses, including Alzheimer's disease.

Poverty

We not only continue to have significant communities of poverty across this wealthy country, but our cities are filled with homeless and destitute individuals and families. In 2003, the number of people in poverty was 35.9 million, up 1.3 million from the previous year. For all children under age eighteen, the poverty rate increased from 16.7 percent in 2002 to 17.6 percent in 2003. The number actually in poverty rose from 12.1 million to 12.9 million.

Some of these individuals, be they residents of rural Maine or the barrios of Los Angeles, are on the federal welfare rolls, while others have fallen through the cracks in the system.

Poverty is not their only problem. Unemployment, substance abuse, illness, and a host of other social ills also can be part of the picture for the social and human services worker fighting the battle of chronic poverty. Fortunately, the professional is not working alone as an agent for change. Government and private programs for jobs, housing, employment, and numerous preventive initiatives try to help as does an enormous network of other professionals.

Juvenile Delinquency

It appears that a variety of risk factors affect whether an adolescent finds his or her way to adulthood without becoming a member of the juvenile justice system. Risk factors include poverty, welfare dependence, absence of one or both parents, marital status of the parents, and educational attainment of the parents. And, according to the Department of Justice and the Office of Juvenile Justice and Delinquency Prevention, once very young offenders enter the system, they are influenced by older deviant juveniles who are housed with them, increasing the likelihood that the very young offenders will continue their delinquent behavior.

We know our penal institutions are not appropriate sites for remediation, and many job-training programs have discovered that to ensure employment they need to provide for follow-through for graduates. Working with juvenile offenders presents great challenges along with the possibility of equally large rewards for the community as well as for the social and human services worker.

Crime

During the early part of this century, all categories of crime reported in the FBI's Crime Index remained steady. In contrast, the total number of prisoners under the jurisdiction of the federal or state adult correctional authorities hit a record high of almost 1.5 million. The debate over punishment versus rehabilitation continues, but in the meantime, social and human services workers play an important role in the justice system. Some work directly with the prison population, while others assist with the reentry of inmates into the community.

Alcohol Abuse

Alcohol abuse remains largely hidden to the majority of the public, but the social and human services worker is all too aware of the pervasiveness of alcoholism and the great sadness and pain it can bring to families, relationships, employment, and, most important, the alcoholics themselves. Alcohol continues to be one of the most costly abused substances. According to the latest information from the National Institute on Alcohol Abuse and Alcoholism, the overall economic cost of alcohol abuse was $185 billion. More is being learned about treatment methods, the impact on children of alcoholic parents, and the role heredity may play in the predisposition to alcoholism. Considerable work is being done on several frontiers for alcohol abusers and their problems, but it remains an enormous social challenge.

Substance Abuse

Substance abuse remains a complex and challenging problem with a multitude of related issues. For the social and human services worker, treating addiction requires the combined forces of both the medical community and other helping professions. According to the National Institute on Drug Abuse (drugabuse.gov/infofacts/nationtrends.html), the use of cocaine/crack, heroin, methamphetamines, Ecstasy, and PCP as well as the misuse of prescription opiates is growing and spreading to populations that previously had not used them. Substance abuse can lead to crime that supports the habit and is as destructive to relationships as alcoholism. Unlike alcohol, however, the number and variety of substances available for abuse is ever-changing and can present difficult challenges to the helping professional when the drug is unknown or unidentifiable.

Following detoxification, self-help programs, halfway houses, mentoring, and individual and group counseling are vital adjunctive therapies for the recovering addict.

Mental Illness

The general public is aware of and conversant in most of the social conditions we've been describing. These issues are on the nightly news and in our morning newspaper. Less understood and more confusing is the world of mental illness. The National Institute of Mental Health (nimh.nih.gov/healthinformation) has reported that four of the ten leading causes of disability in the United States and other developed countries are mental disorders—major depression, bipolar disorder, schizophrenia, and obsessive-compulsive disorder. Many people suffer from more than one mental disorder at a given time.

Mental Retardation

Many people understand the distinction between a mental illness, such as depression, and mental retardation. According to a definition developed by the American Association on Mental Retardation (aamr.org), mental retardation is a disability characterized by significant limitations both in intellectual functioning and in adaptive behavior as expressed in conceptual, social, and practical adaptive skills. This disability originates before age eighteen. Studies have shown that somewhere between 1 percent and 3 percent of Americans have mental retardation. The social and human services worker plays an important role by helping with semi-independent and independent living, employment, and marriage.

Chronic Illness

Social and human services professionals assist individuals living with chronic illnesses and their families. Some of these illnesses include:

Alzheimer's disease
Attention deficit disorder
Autism
Burns
Cancer
Cystic fibrosis
Epilepsy
Heart disease
Juvenile diabetes
Kidney disease
Leukemia
Liver disease
Lung disease
Lupus
Multiple sclerosis
Neurological disorders and stroke

No matter which chronic illness affects an individual, the ongoing physical and often emotional challenges require attention and coordination. These conditions can and do require significant time to manage but need not relegate those affected to marginal lives. Dealing with insurers, caregivers, and service providers can become a preoccupation and can drain an individual of the energy and spirit to accomplish more. As social and human services professionals assemble networks to provide services, opportunities for increasingly normal life patterns emerge for patients, families, and caregivers. This ability to provide an improved quality of life has been both a continuing challenge to professionals in the field and their greatest triumph.

Explore the Range of Issues and Populations Our Society Represents

Although we have described, in some detail, a few of the larger populations receiving social and human services, many other groups are served and issues are addressed. The list of services that follows is just the tip of the iceberg for the graduate looking to enter the social and human services field. Review the list and think about which issues interest you. Some may surprise you, or perhaps you've never heard of others. Each area is worth your exploration, and Internet searches, career books, magazines, and journals can provide you with information that you will find enlightening. In addition, at the end of this chapter we have listed a number of professional organizations that can provide helpful information.

Abortion-alternatives counseling
Abortion counseling
Adoption services
Athletic services
Battered spouses and children's services
Blind, organizations for the
Charity services
Child counseling
Children's services
Chronic disease services
Communicable diseases counseling and services
Community services

Consumer services
Crime victim services
Crisis intervention services
Day-care assistance
Deaf and hearing impaired, services for the
Developmentally disabled persons services
Disabled assistance services
Divorce counseling
Domestic violence counseling
Drug abuse and prevention services
Economic assistance services
Educational information services
Elderly persons services
Ethnic organizations and services
Family and individual services
Foster care services
Gay, lesbian, and transgendered organizations and services
Halfway houses
Health services
Home care services
Homeless persons services
Housing assistance
Human services
Immigrant assistance
Legal counseling
Medical relief services
Mental health services
Men's services
Philanthropic services
Pregnancy and maternity services
Pregnancy counseling and prevention information
Rape crisis services
Religious organizations
Sex information and counseling
Single parents' services
Suicide prevention services
Tenants' services
Travelers' assistance

Vocational services
Volunteer services
Women's services
Youth services

How Can the Psychology Major Fit into the Picture?

What do all of these social services organizations and the people who work in them do? More important, as a psychology major with an undergraduate degree, is there a place for you? For the psychology major interested in social and human services, the problem is not finding one but how to choose among the many types of agencies that do exist. Each involves a world of specialized information, support networks, informational and financial resources, and dedicated professionals and paraprofessionals working to improve the human condition.

Social services are concerned with bringing people together with the information and tools they need to cope with and surmount challenges in their lives. Social services workers help bring harmony to strained lives and circumstances; enrich lives that may be impoverished in any manner of speaking; and teach people the skills and techniques needed so they can continue to find resources, work out solutions, and lead richer, fuller lives.

Any profession that deals with all of humanity and with the infinite number of human issues from birth to death cannot be limited to workers of one educational preparation or one kind of knowledge or experience. When issues as diverse as sexual abuse, disease, mental and physical disabilities, housing, insurance, education, crime, and alcohol abuse are part of the daily menu of problems presented in the environment, a range of educational backgrounds is required.

The field of social services draws from many areas of academic preparation: psychology, religion, counseling, medicine, health and nutrition, home economics, child care, law enforcement, political science, mental health, criminal justice, and, of course, social work. Social services involve seeking out and then connecting clients with the information, materials, and resources they require, followed by providing the assistance and support clients may need to obtain such information and resources. In connecting clients with the many services and agencies providing assistance, the social services worker has a networking, communicating, bridge-building, role-modeling, counseling, and mentoring role.

Definition of the Career Path

Let's begin the discussion of this career path by focusing on some entry-level social and human services want ads:

Housing Specialist (NY, NY). Working in pairs, conduct outreach and identify permanent housing for homeless individuals. Assist clients with understanding housing system. Collect necessary documents to complete application (ID, TB tests, psychiatric evals, etc.). Research appropriate vacancies, secure interviews for clients, and accompany them. Maintain case records and complete administrative duties. B.A./B.S. required in related field. Strong computer, writing, communication, interpersonal skills needed. Experience needed. Bilingual preferred. Salary: $40,000.

Intern (Asheville, NC). Entry-level positions for recent college grads. Spend a year living on campus & rotate through five treatment programs. Work with male & female mental health diagnosed students ages ten to seventeen in residential facility. Gain experience equivalent to two to three years' direct care. Bachelor's in human services–related area (psychology, sociology, criminal justice). $5.15/hour, housing, full-time employee benefits (health, paid leave, etc.).

Women's Advocate (MO). Provide advocacy services to women in shelter & staff hotline. Complete intake procedures, offer support, provide crisis intervention, and address needs of all shelter residents. Maintain client caseload & meet with clients on weekly basis. B.S. in social service field & knowledge of domestic violence. Police background screening required. Competitive salary & benefits.

Information & Referral Counselor (Falls Church, VA). Spanish/Vietnamese language skills required. Counselor responsible for being one of primary points of contact for potential clients seeking services & information. May provide

---

continued

individual case management services. Bachelor's degree in psychology, social work, or other mental/social service field. Some experience required. Competitive salary & benefits.

Volunteer Coordinator (MN). Thirty hrs/wk at $14/hr. Recruit, interview, screen, & select agency volunteers. Supervise volunteers assigned to food shelf, clothes closet, & seasonal projects. Develop & maintain job descriptions for all volunteer positions. Develop & conduct training for volunteers. Take necessary steps to ensure mutually beneficial volunteer assignment. B.A./B.S. in social work or psychology.

In breaking down these want ads into job components, several basic duties emerge: assessing a wide range of conditions, counseling, record keeping, networking, meeting immediate needs, referring, working with volunteers, interacting with multidisciplinary teams, and building a knowledge base. Each job presents some unique circumstances, and so these job components will carry a different weight depending on the position and the setting. Evaluate where your strengths are (you may want to refer back to the self-assessment you completed); this will guide you in choosing the setting in which you may work most effectively.

Assessing a Wide Range of Conditions

The types of human conditions seen in various settings are described in the previous ads. The social and human services worker can expect to become quite adept at recognizing the signs of alcohol abuse, delirium tremens, diabetes, hypothermia, malnutrition, or addiction, and will become skilled at assessing a client's self-help skills and willingness to change.

Counseling

Counseling is the process of connection and deep human involvement between people. Certainly there are many formal schools of counseling theory and technique, but individual counselors ultimately evolve a counseling technique that works for them and their clients. Often, for the clientele of the social and human services worker, the deeply empathic listening attention of the counselor is, in and of itself, therapeutic. Clients who have a caring listener who values them as a person, and to whom they can talk about their problems often can begin down the road to healthy living.

Record Keeping

The social and human services worker must keep excellent records and may sometimes be responsible for helping with financial assistance or other forms of aid. Frequently the social services worker is called upon to explain local, state, or federal regulations or procedures to their clients and may actively assist them in their efforts to secure financial assistance.

Many new entrants into the field of social services work are overwhelmed by the amount of paperwork and telephone work. Hours and hours each day are spent chasing people down by telephone or processing paperwork. Carrying out administrative duties can certainly create doubts about the "service" in social services work.

Networking

The new worker in this job will slowly build a network of contacts that he or she can count on for help in explaining the law; finding long-term housing; in locating job training and employment; and finding sources for food, clothing, medical help, and every other kind of assistance clients require. Social services workers, through their daily networking activities, become very aware of the "hows" and "whys" of their clients' situations and the social fabric that contributes to their problems and the difficulties in solving them.

Meeting Immediate Needs

Social services workers have little time for psychological evaluation, and testing is seldom done. Instead the emphasis is on meeting more immediate and demanding needs, such as shelter, food, and health care. Some clients can be assisted quickly; many others progress very slowly with much recidivism; and, sadly, some clients cannot be helped at all. The rewards are in the clients who can be helped. Social services workers remain in the trenches, each day making a contribution to meeting their clients' immediate needs, and helping those who, if left alone, might not be able to do for themselves.

Referring

An important role for the social services worker is helping clients locate long-term shelters or permanent housing, locate jobs or job training, and secure the sometimes necessary attendant issues, such as day care or clothing. Connecting clients to agencies and resources for many of these basic needs is a first step in the rehabilitative process. Some clients will need counseling and referral to treatment programs before other initiatives can successfully begin.

Each client may need connections with a number of support services. The adult client with cerebral palsy may need help connecting with someone who can advocate for him or her for appropriate and accessible housing. A referral to another agency may provide help in wheelchair maintenance or physical therapy. The client may need assistance in applying for food stamps or simply need a ride to and from the grocery store.

The job involves interviewing clients to assess the number and severity of their problems, making an evaluation, and determining specific needs and how best to satisfy them. The social services worker then brings together all the necessary agencies, individuals, information, and resources to create some positive change. In doing so, he or she will become well acquainted with the police station, local stores, the court system, state aid, criminal elements in their locality, and the drug trade.

Working with Volunteers

Most social and human services organizations simply could not survive without dedicated, caring, and skilled volunteers. The problems are widespread, the need is great, and resources are very thinly spread. Volunteers help to bridge these gaps in service, staffing, and resources, and they do it with enthusiasm and sincere interest.

Volunteers often work only brief hours on irregular schedules. They require training and, as unpaid staff, need to be assigned activities and responsibilities in keeping with these considerations. The social and human services worker will spend some administrative time in scheduling volunteers, training them on a continual basis, and seeking to incorporate them in the organization's mission in a fulfilling manner.

Interacting with a Multidisciplinary Team

The client often receives help from a number of sources simultaneously. He or she may be receiving personal counseling from a therapist for sexual or physical abuse and attending Alcoholics Anonymous meetings daily. You may have a client in personal therapy, in job counseling, undergoing drug rehabilitation, under a physician's care for a chronic illness, and on probation all at the same time. You will have to help clients maintain these commitments and orchestrate the efforts of all these helping agencies to reduce conflict and maintain a reasonable climate for your clients. Very often your clients will not be strong advocates for their own cases; you can work with all of the professionals involved in your clients' care to devise a program that best suits their needs.

Building a Knowledge Base

Reading this, you begin to appreciate the time and focus entry-level social services workers must bring to the job. And, as they improve their job performance (their ability to help), they are acquiring valuable information, knowledge, and skills in the setting and with the population they encounter.

This knowledge base builds almost imperceptibly, aided by in-service training, conferences, seminars, and a daily schedule of clients with their individual case histories. The caseworker finds his or her understanding of "the system" expanding, and the bureaucratic and legal aspects of assistance and support become clearer and more workable. You're becoming a professional. Laws and pending legislation can vary dramatically by state, and there can be differences in implementation within states. To be an effective social and human services worker is to understand the system your clients find themselves in and to act as a guide in securing services for them. To do this well requires making contacts and connections, most often through your individual work for clients and through learning how things work in your locality.

Though you provide helping skills, much of your work depends on making connections with others and in advocating for the support and assistance for your client that the law entitles them to. Understanding and learning the various systems takes time and experience.

Why Psychology Rather than Social Work?

The job listings provided previously give you some sense of the diversity of work present in social services, not only in the kinds of activities a social services worker engages in, but also in the presenting problems of the people they work with and the age and gender mix of those populations. The breadth and scope of social services work and its initiatives result in an equally broad selection of candidates for jobs.

What you probably took special notice of in these ads was the fairly generalized degree demands, in most cases, a bachelor's degree in psychology or some reasonably related field. Most employers, for obvious reasons, would prefer previous experience so that the job candidate already understands the work and is familiar with the issues of clients.

While the generalized requirements may please some, other job seekers may be skeptical. Why don't employers demand a social work degree? How can they be so loose in job qualifications when the work is so important? The answers lie in the nature of social services work. It is enormously demanding, many would say taxing, of the social services worker's energy, patience, time, and physical resources. Although the field has a range of pay for similar jobs, depending upon the employment setting, high salaries have not been a tradition of the social and human services field. The short answer may be that hiring officials who fill tough jobs paying less than top wages must draw from a wide pool of applicants.

There's another, equally valid, reason. When you look at the spectrum of problems social services workers must wrestle with and the diversity of the human canvas that is placed before them, it is difficult to know where the talent may lie to help alleviate some of the struggle. Certainly, we have social workers who have studied the issues and earned a degree in the subject on the bachelor's, master's, and doctoral level. Others come to these same issues and concerns with as much to offer but a different, yet equally valuable, preparation in other academic areas and life experiences.

How Can the Social and Human Services Worker Grow?

Some students contemplating a career in social and human services wonder whether they can sustain a lifelong career in this field. They worry about burnout. You can make three specific efforts as you begin your career that will help you keep this issue in perspective. First, think about whether the skills and the knowledge base you are building can be transferred to other populations and settings. Second, consider preparing for growth in a specialty. And third, take care of your own career needs.

Transferring Your Skills and Knowledge

One way you can progress in your career is to change work settings. You can consciously create some meaningful transitions by learning which skills and knowledge are valued in a given workplace. Some of the skills and knowledge that you acquire as you begin your career will be directly transferable to a different situation, while others will not relate to different settings. Look for the common threads. A position assisting homeless adults would provide some good experience in working with an elderly population, and that work can relate to a number of other, more stable eldercare situations. Or, work in adult substance abuse might prove sufficient to merit a move into an adolescent substance abuse clinic. Be aware, however, that the type of facility and the type of client has changed, so fewer skills and less knowledge are transferable. A move from a facility servicing homeless adults to a residential center caring for child victims of sexual or physical abuse, for instance, would be more difficult to make.

Preparing for Growth in a Specialty

You can also grow and develop in social and human services work by building a specific body of knowledge and helping skills; that, by necessity, suggests working with a particular population and learning the resources that exist for that group until you are proficient. Job growth may then come in the form of more supervisory responsibility for other caregivers, management control of a facility, or advanced or specialized education in your field.

Taking Care of Your Own Career Needs

It's no mystery that social and human services workers burn out. It's a tough, tough job, and some professionals simply get weary of the obstacles put in their clients' way or the recidivism among clients whom they have tried mightily to help make some headway against serious obstacles.

You may act tired, get cynical, or want a job that is less physically and emotionally draining. Changing the population you work with is certainly one technique to combat burnout, especially if many of the issues are familiar ones to you. Growing within your specialty and taking an administrative or management position is yet another option.

Whatever you decide to do, make it an active choice. Don't let your career just "happen." You don't want your boss to take you aside one day and suggest you're overextended, tired, and no longer effective. Take your own career pulse from time and time and ask yourself, "Hey, how am I doing?" If you feel you need something different, make it your choice. Social and human services is a noble calling with rich rewards, but it makes equally insistent demands on your time and energy.

Working Conditions

Social services workers at every level of expertise (doctorate, master's, bachelor's, and paraprofessional) are employed in a number of different settings. The setting, in large part, dictates the types of activities the social services worker engages in, the jobs and duties he or she has, the types of clients and client that will be encountered, and the ways in which the worker will practice his or her social services profession.

Some specific issues to consider include:

- Age of the population served
- Source of funding for the agency/service
- Working hours
- Specific issues of the clientele
- Personal safety

Age of the Population Served

Your interest in working with children, or your care and compassion for the elderly, may have been what drew you to work in social and human services. Many agencies serve specific age populations, so if age of your clientele is an important condition, be sure to target the appropriate agencies.

Some services are structured for particular age groups, so the activities, therapies, and atmosphere will combine to say to the client, "This is a for-you service." Shelters for adolescent males or senior centers are good examples. Other services are age blind and are built around a condition, disease entity, or problem. The HIV virus is age blind and a service supporting those afflicted would span all ages.

Source of Funding for the Agency/Service

The stability of funding is an important consideration for any helping service. Funds that are not stable—that perhaps need to be renewed each year—can create a sense of impermanence affecting staff morale and services if refunding is delayed.

Other agencies may have relatively stable funding but require significant development work to continually raise money and will call upon the social services worker to assist in these fund-raising efforts. While necessary to continued viability, this fund-raising work can often be an additional burden on already overworked staff.

Some grant-funded programs ultimately end or program funding slowly decreases and programs are disbanded, leaving workers to seek new employment. Other effects of inconsistent or decreasing funding sources can be seen on the physical facilities, location, supplies, and quality of staff.

Working Hours

Social services providers work many different shifts and schedules, especially in the areas of homelessness, drug and substance abuse, and sheltered care. There may be standard rotating shifts or three full days on and four days off. There may be sleep-in accommodations with a need to be available twenty-four hours. There are traditional thirty-seven-hour weeks as well. You'll need to consider working hours carefully and think about how they will affect your personal life, relationships, avocational interests, and well-being.

Specific Issues of the Clientele

Some substance abusers steal to support their habits. Many adolescent men and women have unprotected sex before marriage. Street people may sell their blood so they can buy alcohol. The list of problems and behaviors goes on and on. Some of these may be inconsistent with your own value system.

Your clients need help, not judgment. As you explore possible work settings, it is important for you to ascertain how you feel about the issues facing the people with whom you choose to work. Your clients need compassion, caring, a sense of humor, and hopefulness, not lectures, censorship, or condemnation. Determine for yourself where you can be the most helpful and where you can commit to those you hope to serve.

Personal Safety

When people encounter great hardship and struggle in their lives, it can have pronounced effects on their temperaments. Anger, hostility, and violence may lie close to the surface, and from time to time, there certainly have been incidences involving threats to the personal safety of social and human services workers.

Most professionals would assure you that this is not a dominant concern in their workday lives. They exercise caution in their client relationships; they share concerns with coworkers; and they activate response systems, including police, if threats occur. In some settings, such as abortion clinics, overnight shelters, or disaster relief situations, tempers flare and outbreaks of violence may occur. In most cases, skilled personnel are well equipped to deal with this and do so effectively.

Think about your own ability to tolerate conflict and mediate violence. Consider your personal physical characteristics and the population you are interested in serving, and talk to professionals now working in these areas for the best advice on how to cope with threats to your physical safety.

Network to Get Information and Answers

Because of your educational background in psychology and your interest in relating that education directly to social services, it's especially important for you to take the time to talk to some practitioners, even if their academic preparation was different from your own. Talking to people "in the field" will provide a reality check that no amount of reading can duplicate. It will bring home some truths about the job that you might not have expected.

Think carefully and examine your own interests, skills, and attributes before committing to a particular type of service. The self-assessment in Chapter 1 provides a strong beginning for your exploration. Further talks with career professionals both in your career-counseling center and among the social service community will help you decide if certain client groups and their associated challenges are interesting enough for you to work with as a career or at least to begin your career.

Training and Qualifications

Review both the personal and professional qualifications we have outlined in this section and decide how they fit with what you have to offer.

Personal Qualifications

Communicative
Concern for others
Dedicated
Discreet
Effective speaker
Empathic
Ethical
Good listener
Good with people
High standards
Idealistic
Independent
Innovative
Mature
Objective
Productive
Realistic
Resilient
Respectful
Responsible
Responsive
Sense of humor

Sensitive
Stable
Teacher
Thoughtful
Writer

Social and human services work is so diverse that it would be foolish to try and create a comprehensive list of necessary personal characteristics. This long list just suggests of the personal characteristics that your profession will draw upon to a greater or lesser degree. The counseling techniques that may be effective in establishing rapport with young, unwed mothers may not serve the social services worker in good stead when dealing with the chronically mentally ill. But there are some well-understood qualities described in this section that are needed in many, many social and community services positions. The psychology major considering a career in social and human services needs to review the following list and rate himself or herself on these criteria.

Concern for Others. One must be concerned for people and their problems. To engage the client and to assess the situation, the social services worker needs empathy, sensitivity, an ability to establish and maintain rapport, and an appreciation of the wonderful diversity present in our population.

Working with a frustrated adolescent may require sitting with him or her for more than an hour before he or she begins to open up and talk to you about current problems. An elderly patient may share fears and concerns more easily if you begin by letting the client show you a family album or favorite pictures.

Appropriate Detachment. While concern for others is important, to be effective you must have a maturity and ability to distance yourself enough to not take on others' problems as your own. The social and human services professional will find no paucity of clients and many with problems that seem almost insurmountable. The work goes on and on, and sometimes progress is very slow.

For that reason, professionals need to pace themselves. They need to respect their own limitations and what they can accomplish. If you are exhausted and overwrought, allowing clients to call you at home or interfere with your personal life, you will eventually self-extinguish. What help can you be to your clients and to the system if you are suffering from burnout?

True professionals in this field know their limitations and understand the importance of leaving work at work. They appreciate their own need for rejuvenation and restoration each day to be able to return to and be effective at work. Clients have problems you can help with, but they are not your problems.

Ability to Work the System. Social services workers must be quick studies in political systems to be able to marshal the necessary resources to help solve clients' problems. Referral networks, sources of financial aid, and housing entitlements all have their hierarchies, paperwork, and influential personalities. To do your best for your clients is to understand not only how the system "should" work, but how, in fact, it does work.

Flexibility. Flexibility is another key personal trait needed in social and human services work. Work hours or shifts may change constantly, the physical location where you carry out your duties may move, and members of a multidisciplinary team may be constantly changing given different schedule rotations. Assess your ability to be happy with the level of flexibility required for the types of positions you are considering and the types of populations you would be working with.

Professional Qualifications

Preprofessional and professional positions in social and human services work are largely determined by degree level and type of degree. Preprofessional positions are typically filled by workers with no degree or those with an associate's degree who are acting as aides or assistants to social and human services workers. Professional positions include jobs where the individual has at least a bachelor's degree in psychology, social work, or sociology that will satisfy the social services agency's needs.

Licensure/Certification. Workers in the social and human services field have come under increasing public scrutiny. As in any area of human endeavor, there have been scandals and examples of unethical behavior. Laws and regulations surrounding the provision of services have increased exponentially, and many professional organizations publish detailed ethical guidelines for their members.

In addition to advanced degree attainment as an outward mark of professionalism, both licensure and certification requirements exist in many states. Licensure ensures that certain educational standards and experiential standards have been met. It often involves some type of written examination and helps the public know the individual has met some state-mandated criteria for professionalism. Licensing boards are then able to discipline unethical or fraudulent practitioners by revoking this license.

Certification through professional organizations promotes standards of education, practice, accountability, discretion, ethics, and visibility, and helps assure the public that the individual employee has met some established standards. Certification can involve testing or the documentation of professional development and years of practice. It is often issued for a limited period of time and then requires renewal.

See your career office or check state websites for information on licensure, and applicable professional associations for certification information.

Knowledge of Other Languages. Frequently, an urban or metropolitan job announcement in social and human services will request fluency in Spanish, Chinese, Vietnamese, Cambodian, or another language indicative of the growing immigrant communities in these areas. While the record of assimilation, especially in language acquisition, among these new citizens is remarkable, new arrivals and the elderly often cannot be effectively served without communicating in their native tongue.

Earnings

People interested in working in social and human services will take an interesting journey when trying to learn more about starting salaries. There is solid information on the earning levels of doctoral-level psychologists, but what can the newly degreed psychology graduate with limited experience hope to earn working in social and human services? The answer comes in part from looking at a wide variety of actual job listings in social and human services. The Bureau of Labor Statistics (bls.gov) indicates that a starting salary might be as low as $20,000 to $22,000. We know that wages vary depending on the size of the employer and the geographic region of the country. When we examined nongovernment job listings showing the starting wage, they ranged from $5.15 per hour plus housing for an internship in a small city to $40,000 in one of the nation's largest metropolitan areas. Federal government jobs for recent college graduates offer a base salary starting at slightly more than $30,000. So begin networking to get a solid understanding of the wages paid in the geographic area where you want to work and for the type of work you hope to undertake. Because wages may be lower than you anticipated, be sure to complete the Calculate Your Economic Needs portion of the self-assessment to verify that you will be able to meet your basic economic needs.

Career Outlook

Regrettably, the problems that face society do not abate, and each generation seems to encounter new and more challenging issues, such as the spread of AIDS and random acts of violence. In addition, natural disasters, terrorist acts, and other uncontrollable events occur without warning, causing tremendous damage to people's lives and well-being. Each type of problem precipitates the need for a core of services and a host of other support mechanisms.

Affordable health care, housing, and food should be controllable, but they remain out of reach for many people and with dire consequences. Social and human services workers will continue to be needed to help connect these people with services that are available to them.

The U.S. Department of Labor, Bureau of Labor Statistics projects that the demand for social and human services workers will grow faster than the average through the year 2012. Fast-growing occupations generally have good employment prospects and conditions favorable for advancement.

Strategy for Finding the Jobs

As a psychology major interested in social and human services, you can undertake six tasks to enhance your job search. Be ready to:

- Identify the social concerns that interest you the most
- Become very familiar with the required professional qualifications
- Identify the personal qualifications you possess
- Build skills and gain direct experience with a population that interests you
- Network with professionals working in the field
- Relate your psychology background to what the employer needs

Undertaking these activities, along with the other phases of the job search as outlined in Part One, will put you on the right track as you begin to establish your career.

Identify the Social Concerns That Interest You the Most

As you have seen in reading this career path, many issues and concerns are addressed in social and human services work. You may have been drawn to major in psychology because of your deep interest in helping children or in promoting a cause, such as affordable housing for all who seek it. No matter what your interests are, there are many, many places for the psychology major in social and human services, but only you can determine where you want to begin your career. This choice will help you create a focused résumé, select appropriate employment sites to investigate, and interview in an effective way. You'll be able to relate your history to what the employer needs in a potential worker.

Become Very Familiar with the Required Professional Qualifications

Your job search begins with an in-depth awareness of the types and levels of skills and abilities that are really needed in social and human services work. In the job announcements we have presented for this path, we have seen requirements for workers such as experience with a specific population, creativity, budget experience, the ability to teach survival skills, flexibility, the ability to work effectively on a multidisciplinary team, motivation, a high level of energy, planning ability, implementation skills, and facilitator skills.

Begin to match your skills and experience with those that many employers will need. For instance, you may have worked effectively on a food service team, you may have taught a lifesaving skill such as cardiopulmonary resuscitation, or you may have helped a professor plan a regional meeting. It is your job to make those experiences relevant to a social services employer.

Identify the Personal Qualifications You Possess

In the Training and Qualifications section of this chapter, we discussed some personal traits that the social and human services worker should possess. Those included concern for others, appropriate detachment, an ability to work the system, and flexibility. You may want to create a résumé that allows you to highlight the qualifications you possess and can offer an employer. A modified résumé that includes a capabilities section allows you to enhance the way a potential employer reads and understands your relevant experience. For example, you might indicate on your résumé capabilities such as:

- Empathic communicator
- Effective resource provider
- Flexible team member

The employer then would read your work history section and look for the experience you've had that allowed you to build these skills.

Build Skills and Gain Direct Experience with a Population That Interests You

Review the actual job listings shown in Definition of the Career Path. Two of the ads ask specifically for experience. You can begin gaining this experience through some combination of the following: volunteer work, part-time work, full-time summer work, and internships. It will be important for you to get some hands-on experience as soon as you realize you are interested in social and human services work. You will get to test the waters to see if the work is a good fit given your interests and abilities, and you'll have that all-important experience to put on your résumé.

If you are seeking volunteer work, it's certainly not hard to find. Review the list of social services organizations in the yellow pages (online or print version), and contact these organizations to see what their volunteer needs are and what training they provide. This can be a great way to enhance your skill base at no cost. These same organizations may also offer employment opportunities. Be sure to start your search early; there will be lots of competition for these jobs. If an internship is the type of experience you are looking for, check with the head of your psychology department and with your career office to find out about the opportunities available to you. Deadlines come early for some internships, so don't put off the research necessary to find them.

Network with Professionals Working in the Field

No one can give you a more accurate accounting of what social and human services work is really like than a professional currently employed in the field. Start with the faculty in your psychology department and see whom they can recommend. You should also check with the career office and see who in your college or university alumni network may be a good source of information given your interests. Review the description of networking provided in Chapter 3, and carefully prepare to get the most you can out of this experience.

Relate Your Psychology Background to What the Employer Needs

As you progressed in your degree program, you took course work that provided you with specific knowledge and skills that are valuable in the workplace. You may have decided you were interested in working with victims of crime through a parole authority. Well, that introductory course you took in criminal justice that helped you gain a deeper understanding of the criminal justice system, combined with your course work in abnormal behavior, gave you a background that will allow you to more effectively serve the victims of crime with whom you would be working. Generalize this example and see how your course work relates to the population you want to serve. Consider adding a Related Course Work section to your résumé, one that will pleasantly surprise the employer with additional knowledge you have added to your background.

Possible Employers

In considering social and human services work, you should investigate a range of employers. As a starting point for your job search, seven types of employers are reviewed. Be sure to add to the list as you review actual job listings.

1. Nonprofit agencies
2. Medical/health organizations
3. Federal/state/local governmental agencies
4. Corrections and rehabilitation
5. Insurance companies
6. Religious organizations
7. Retirement homes/communities

Nonprofit Agencies

Nonprofit agencies offer an incredibly wide array of social and human services, and each hires workers to provide, oversee, administer, and manage these services. They need you, the psychology major, on their staffs. Whether you're working in consumer services, aid to the homeless, or immigration assistance, your skills in counseling, record keeping, and service referrals will be critical to your success.

Help in Locating These Employers. One excellent resource you will want to use to begin your job search is socialservices.com. This website lists positions involving mental health, substance abuse, children and youth, medical social work, criminal justice, domestic violence, community organizing and outreach, homelessness, and many others. The New Social Worker Online career center (socialworker.com) has links to a variety of job listings, not all of which require a degree in social work. A volume worth looking through is *Careers in Social and Rehabilitation Services*. And don't forget to check the yellow pages under Social and Human Services for a listing of agencies in a given geographic area.

Medical/Health Organizations

These types of facilities serve a range of clients and assist them with issues relating to, among others, alcohol and chemical dependency, rape and violence, family planning, hospice care, health, or AIDS. The knowledge and skills you've built could be put to use in any of these settings. If, for instance, you were an AIDS outreach worker and your clients were young women seeking family planning counseling, you would use your specialized knowledge in working with these clients to educate them about the disease and work with those who had the disease to help them receive available medical as well as other services.

Help in Locating These Employers. To gain valuable insights into working in the medical/health field, review the books *Career Opportunities in Health Care* and *America's Top Medical, Education & Human Services Jobs* and two resources you'll find in larger libraries, *Encyclopedia of Medical Organizations and Agencies* and the *Medical and Health Information Directory*. These references provide specific information on job listings and potential employers that you can use to enhance your job search.

Federal/State/Local Governmental Agencies

Some social and human services workers are employed in corrections and public assistance departments. Corrections departments are growing faster than other areas of government, so social and human services workers should find job opportunities increasing. Public assistance programs also have been employing more social and human services workers with bachelor's degrees in an attempt to avoid employing workers with more education who demand higher pay.

The U.S. government worker category that most closely resembles the social and human services work described in this chapter is GS-0101 Social Science, Psychology, and Welfare Series. Several relevant job groupings fall within this category, including correctional treatment specialists, social insurance administrators, unemployment insurance specialists, health insurance administrators, psychologists, social workers, and social services workers.

Entry-level federal positions for college graduates are classified at the GS-7 or GS-9 level.

Help in Locating These Employers. Two volumes to start with are *Career Opportunities in Politics, Government, and Activism* and *Opportunities in Government Careers*. Actual job listings for state jobs can be found on the Web by searching state._.us. Just insert in the blank the two-letter abbreviation for the state you want to explore. Then look for a link to state job listings. To look for U.S. government jobs, visit the Office of Personnel Management website at usajobs.opm.gov. This site explains the federal employment process and lets you get general information, look at current job openings, and submit an online application.

Corrections and Rehabilitation (Federal, State, Local)

Social services workers in corrections and rehabilitation at all governmental levels may have job titles such as child welfare caseworker, clinical psychologist, corrections counselor, parole officer, recreation leader, or social group worker. Psychology majors who (1) have taken related course work or have an academic minor in a field such as criminal justice and (2) have gained direct work experience (internship, part-time job, summer job, volunteer work) would be eligible for many of these types of positions.

Help in Locating These Employers. Several books provide a starting point for your exploration of a career in corrections and rehabilitation. *Opportunities in Law Enforcement & Criminal Justice Careers* and *Great Jobs for Criminal Justice Majors* are excellent starting points. Use an Internet search engine and enter keywords that interest you, e.g., "criminal justice" and "job," and you'll be directed to a variety of sites listing job openings. You also can use information in the previous section to find current job listings.

Insurance Companies

Many health insurers provide managed health-care services to their members, and they employ psychology majors to fill positions in customer service, claims, and provider relations. You probably won't meet face-to-face with your clients, but you will assist them in obtaining the physical and mental health services to which they are entitled.

For a large employee benefit program, you might serve as a telemarketing resource, using computerized directory information to provide referrals to individuals seeking assistance. This is a sophisticated position, requiring excellent listening and questioning skills to determine need and the ability to quickly locate information on treatment options.

Help in Locating These Employers. *Career Opportunities in Health Care* and *Career Opportunities in Banking, Finance, and Insurance* provide useful information on starting a career in the insurance industry. The Association of Health Insurance Advisors (ahia.net) website posts jobs, and you can check out other job listings by using your favorite search engine.

Religious Organizations

Many religious organizations offer services to the community and provide trained and qualified personnel to assist those who ask for help. The organization may provide some type of center, or settlement house, where youth can come to use a gym or homeless people can come to sleep. Not all of the workers have specific religious training, although many of them do.

Help in Locating These Employers. Two resources that identify service agencies are *Yearbook of American and Canadian Churches* and *Our Sunday Visitors Catholic Almanac*. Or go online to americanchurchlist.com, which lists both Canadian and American churches. You can access YMCA job listings by searching from the national website (ymca.net) or visiting Y facilities in the cities where you're thinking of working. Jewish Community Center job listings can be accessed at jccworks.com.

Retirement Homes/Communities

If you are interested in working in a retirement home or community, you can follow a couple of different paths. You may want to work in a counseling setting and you might be called a social worker, volunteer coordinator, leisure counselor, or rehabilitation counselor. Or, you may want to play an administrative role, in which case the job titles to look for are housing project manager, site coordinator, or administrator.

Help in Locating These Employers. The American Association of Homes and Services for the Aging posts some job listings on its website (aahsa.org/careers/job_mart/available.asp#market). In addition, you can search for facilities that are members of this organization. Navigate to aahsa.org/consumer _info/homes_svcs_directory/default.asp and then enter search information to obtain the name and address of the member facilities in a given state. *Opportunities in Gerontology and Aging Services Careers* also contains valuable information relating to careers in gerontology that the psychology major may be interested in pursuing. Don't overlook a handy resource—your local yellow pages. It lists retirement and life care communities and homes in specific geographic regions that you can contact about employment.

Possible Job Titles

You will see a wide variety of job titles associated with social and human services. Sometimes the word *counselor* is in the job title, and oftentimes these are considered entry-level positions. For those workers who have more experience, and for you that might mean part-time or summer employment or an internship, the word *coordinator* might be used. Workers who have case management experience or who are responsible for supervision of other workers, facilities, or budgets will often have *manager, director,* or *supervisor* in their job title. Review the titles shown below and look for job listings that match your level of experience.

Care manager
Case coordinator
Case manager
Clinical coordinator
Clinical supervisor
Clinician
Community services specialist
Community support clinician
Consultant
Counseling coordinator
Day treatment clinician
Domestic violence community educator
Family counselor
Health-care representative
Housing specialist
Information and referral counselor
Intensive case manager
Juvenile case manager
Mental health clinician
Mental retardation and mental health counselor
Milieu counselor
Parent counselor/educator
Prevention counselor

Program coordinator
Program director
Program manager
Project manager
Regional support coordinator
Rehabilitation counselor
Social worker
Substance abuse counselor
Women's advocate
Youth counselor

Related Occupations

Many of the occupations that relate to social and human services work draw on the same talents and skills, but some also require a more specialized education than a bachelor's degree in psychology, or they may require certification or licensure. If any of the job titles shown below interest you, consult the *Occupational Outlook Handbook* (bls.gov/oco) for details.

Activity leader
Admissions evaluator
Art therapist
Employment services worker
Expressive therapist
Health club manager
Labor relations manager
Music therapist
Occupational therapist
Physical therapist
Regulatory administrator
Religious worker
Social worker
Volunteer coordinator

Professional Associations

Because social and human services work takes place in such a variety of settings, we provide just an introduction to a smorgasbord of possible professional associations. Contact those having titles that reflect populations you are interested in working with. Use your favorite online search engine, the *Encyclopedia of Associations* at a larger library, or other references we have named to get additional information about why these associations exist and how they can help job seekers and their members.

American Association for Health Education, a member organization of the American Alliance for Health, Physical Education, Recreation, and Dance
1900 Association Dr.
Reston, VA 20191
aahperd.org

American Association of the Deaf-Blind
814 Thayer Ave., Suite 302
Silver Spring, MD 20910
aadb.org

American Association of Homes and Services for the Aging
2519 Connecticut Ave. NW
Washington, DC 20008
aahsa.org

American Association of Retired Persons
601 E St. NW
Washington, DC 20049
aarp.org

American Association on Mental Retardation
444 N. Capitol St. NW, Suite 846
Washington, DC 20001-1512
aamr.org

American Council of the Blind
1155 15th St. NW, Suite 1004
Washington, DC 20005
acb.org

American Society of Criminology
1314 Kinnear Rd.
Columbus, OH 43212
asc41.com

American Society of Directors of Volunteer Services of the American Hospital Association
One N. Franklin, 27th Floor
Chicago, IL 60606
asdvs.org

Association for Conflict Resolution
1015 18th St. NW, Suite 1150
Washington, DC 20036
acrnet.org

Consumer Federation of America
1424 16th St. NW, Suite 604
Washington, DC 20036
consumerfed.org

Disability Rights Education and Defense Fund
2212 6th St.
Berkeley, CA 94710
dredf.org

Housing Assistance Council
1025 Vermont Ave. NW, Suite 606
Washington, DC 20005
ruralhome.org

National Abortion Federation
1755 Massachusetts Ave. NW, Suite 600
Washington, DC 20036
prochoice.org

National Adoption Center
1500 Walnut St., Suite 701
Philadelphia, PA 19102
adopt.org

National Association for Family Child Care
5202 Pinemont Dr.
Salt Lake City, UT 84123
nafcc.org

National Association for Home Care & Hospice
228 7th St. SE
Washington, DC 20003
nahc.org

National Association of Councils on Developmental Disabilities
225 Reinekers Lane, Suite 650-B
Alexandria, VA 22314
nacdd.org

National Association of Public Child Welfare Administrators
c/o American Public Human Services Association
810 1st St. NE, Suite 500
Washington, DC 20002
aphsa.org

National Association of Social Workers
750 1st St. NE, Suite 700
Washington, DC 20002
naswdc.org

National Association of State Alcohol and Drug Abuse Directors
808 17th St. NW, Suite 410
Washington, DC 20006
nasadad.org

National Center for Suicide Prevention Training
55 Chapel St.
Newton, MA 02458
ncspt.org

National Coalition for the Homeless
2201 P St. NW
Washington, DC 20037
nationalhomeless.org

National Coalition for Lesbian, Gay, Bisexual, and Transgender Health
1407 S St. NW
Washington, DC 20009
lgbthealth.net

National Council on Child Abuse and Family Violence
1025 Connecticut Ave. NW, Suite 1012
Washington, DC 20036
nccafv.org

National Immigration Law Center
3435 Wilshire Blvd., Suite 2850
Los Angeles, CA 90010
nilc.org

National Legal Aid and Defender Association
1140 Connecticut Ave. NW, Suite 900
Washington, DC 20036
nlada.org

National Mental Health Association
2001 N. Beauregard St., 12th Floor
Alexandria, VA 22311
nmha.org

National Organization for Women
P.O. Box 1848
Merrifield, VA 22116
now.org

Office for Victims of Crimes
U.S. Department of Justice
810 7th St. NW
Washington, DC 20531
ojp.usdoj.gov/ovc

Single Parent Resource Center
141 W. 28th St., Suite 302
New York, NY 10001
http://singleparentresources.com

U.S. Conference of City Human Services Officials
1620 Eye St. NW, 4th Floor
Washington, DC 20006
usmayors.org/humanservices

World Medical Relief
11745 Rosa Parks Blvd.
Detroit, MI 48206
worldmedicalrelief.com

Young America's Foundation
F. M. Kirby Freedom Center
110 Elden St.
Herndon, VA 20170
yaf.org

8

Path 3:
Human Resources

Many students of psychology feel that the human resources area of business and industry holds a strong application for their undergraduate degree. If you are among this group, explore what this field has to offer, and what values, skills, and abilities it requires of its employees.

Human resources professionals are drawn from a number of undergraduate academic backgrounds, including psychology. An undergraduate degree in psychology does not necessarily provide an advantage in seeking human resources employment; it has more to do with the student's understanding of the human resources function in business and the orientation of the student's academic preparation in psychology. As with so many liberal arts degrees, the degree itself does not suggest any special preparedness, and most employers will make no assumptions about the relevance of a candidate's degree to a potential job opening.

The Human Resources Function in Corporations

The workplace in general and the human resources function in particular are primarily concerned with three types of development that create a cohesive workforce and achieve the overall organizational mission and goals:

1. Training and professional development, or developing key competencies in workers that enable them to carry out their duties
2. Organizational development, which primarily focuses on helping groups manage change

3. Career development, which involves helping employees manage their careers within the organization

Training and Professional Development

Most workers want to be proud of what they accomplish during the work-day, and while they have the basic skills to do a good job, they may need additional training to be able to work at their full potential. A computer data-entry worker may need to learn database management. A new supervisor may need to develop some conflict negotiation skills. The human resources pro-fessional is responsible for making sure that employees either have or are able to develop the competencies they need to do the work they are assigned.

Organizational Development

Organizations are undergoing stressful levels of change to mainsail their strategic advantage in the marketplace. Whether the organization is a non-profit that coordinates emergency relief efforts or a for-profit manufacturer producing the latest in computer chip technology, both have a need for employees who can handle changing needs. The human resources depart-ment can help effect these changes through hiring procedures, employee training, and employee transitions within the organization.

Career Development

Job seekers face an ever-changing marketplace, one that demands flexibility to be able to handle organizational change. Human resources personnel help employees take concrete and specific steps to manage their own career within the organization so that each person can produce work that allows him or her to use a full range of skills and abilities to meet the organizational goals.

Psychology as an Academic Preparation for Human Resources

Whether your college or university offers a standard, broad-based exposure to the discipline of psychology or concentration options in areas such as child or adult development, mental health, counseling psychology, or research design, your best bet would be to take those courses or elect those programs seen as most relevant to a human resources function. These would include all areas of adult development, learning, personality, and social psychology. For instance, abnormal psychology, a popular concentration, would not hold particular relevance for a career in human resources; the workplace as a social organization relies on appropriate behavior. While some human resources programs do offer employee assistance programs (referrals and outplacement to helping professionals for individuals struggling with personal problems), it is not the province of the human resources area to either diagnose or treat these ailments.

Your academic program in psychology also has helped you build a critical set of transferable skills that are highly valued in human resources. You mastered them in the context of studying psychology, but now you must make them relevant to the human resources employer. These skills include your ability to set objectives, evaluate, coach, interview, manage time, write, manage projects, master computer technology, and plan. Each of these skills is critical to functioning effectively in human resources.

"Human resources" is an apt description because this area manages the resource of human productivity for the organization. Psychology could be an excellent preparation for a career in this area if you understand both how your degree will be used and the job you'll be doing.

Whom Does Human Resources Serve?

The essential dilemma for human resources professionals is whom do they serve: the organization or the worker? In the overwhelming majority of circumstances, the answer is the organization, by maintaining the organization's expectations. In areas such as job design, pay grades and classifications, promotion and job enhancement, training and development, benefits administration, and the arbitration of grievances and employee policies, human resources professionals are not advocates of the employee but rather representatives of the employer, exercising the employer's mandate in the administration of the workforce.

However, that does not prohibit the human resources professional from also being an advocate for the worker. Workers who grow in their jobs need to be reclassified to a higher rank. Often this happens because of, and aided by, the policies and encouragement of human resources professionals. Human resources personnel design creative and innovative programs for workers that not only improve their work performance and relationships but extend their influence to all aspects of life. Depending on their size and breadth, human resources programs can touch on life changes, retirement, aging, and many other life issues.

Is Human Resources Really Your Interest?

This discussion brings up an issue that should be of real interest to all psychology majors contemplating human resources work. If your interest in psychology is in human behavior, especially how individuals respond in groups, then human resources work may be of interest.

Maybe cognitive theory is your real interest. If so, research may hold more fruitful jobs for you. If you have studied psychology out of a love for and interest in developing and nurturing the human psyche, you might find a better fit in the areas of social and human services or therapy.

Though there's no doubt many of us credit wonderful opportunities for growth and personal and professional development to the programs and offerings of our human resources department, this is not all the work they do. Sit with a human resources professional and talk about the amount of hostility they endure each day from employees angry over benefits administration or changes in work conditions, salary negotiations, or promotion opportunities. Hear the complaints and humiliation of a discharged employee who must be accompanied by a human resources official as he or she is checked out of every department (security, parking, credit union) before being discharged. There is the challenge of having to remove an employee with the help of security forces. To have the full picture of this "people" job, you need to hear both the positive and the negative.

Definition of the Career Path

Paying close attention to the news for even as little as a week's time will give you a very clear picture of the difficulties of the workplace today and the implications for human resources professionals. Repetitive motion injuries afflict more and more workers using various kinds of equipment. Gender issues are very much alive, with continuing data on inequality in pay as well as abusive and discriminatory behavior toward women. At the same time, the white male no longer dominates the workforce, and human resources professionals must build organizations from an increasingly diverse ethnic, racial, and religious population. There are corresponding challenges to assimilation, inclusion, and tolerance. Human resources professionals try to create understanding and, hopefully, appreciation and enjoyment of this diversity.

Your scrutiny of the news also may have made you aware of a large number of lawsuits between employers and employees. Issues of harassment, discrimination, illegal firings and layoffs, and workplace injury and stress have escalated recently and mean additional challenges for those working in the human resources area. Each lawsuit means documents are subpoenaed from human resources. They may include personnel files, records of vacation or sick days, training opportunities, formal commendations or reprimands, and many other kinds of data. This can add a tremendous burden to an already busy office.

Economics plays a large part in determining the fate of some organizations and you no doubt will have encountered stories of organizations moving their offices across town, across the country, or even out of the country. This has a profound impact on workers and their families. Likewise, many firms have reduced their staffs dramatically in an effort to stay viable and reduce costs.

Some potential employees are more aggressively interested in the economic health of any organization they may be employed by and corresponding benefits that will be provided if they are let go. Employees no longer believe they will be with the same firm for the rest of their lives, and they also recognize the possibility that the organization may be bought or fail. Many want to know from human resources what contingency plans are in effect for any of these situations. Will there be severance pay, outplacement services, counseling, relocation assistance, or transfers to a subsidiary?

The possibility of job loss and frequent job change means workers will be more aggressive in extracting benefits and training and development opportunities from current employers. Human resources personnel may encounter increased and insistent demands for training and development opportunities, college courses, and spousal benefits. Employees as a group may demand resource acquisitions (ergonomic consultations, blood pressure checks, diet counseling, gym or weight room) and an accounting from the organization's management on money spent on staff development. As workers realize a need to be always ready to acquire new skills in preparation for new jobs, they will be more aggressive in using every benefit opportunity. Use of benefits increases the work of human resources in administration and processing and the cost to the organization.

Health-care issues dominate the press and, as the United States struggles with providing effective and economic health care, there will be dramatic effects on the workforce and the employer. Because every change of employee is costly in out-processing a former employee and in-processing and training new talent, human resources professionals have much to be concerned about if worker stability can no longer be tied to health benefits.

In addition, organizations are subtly affected in a positive way by the core of long-term employees who have experienced some history with the organization and have learned to work together as a team. If that team breaks up beyond a critical point, some of that efficiency and networking will be lost, to the detriment of the organization's ability to function most effectively.

Working Conditions

For a job that supposedly involves people (the "humans" in human resources!), a lot of paperwork and data manipulation need to be completed. In examining working conditions in the human resources area, it's best to look at the overall mission of a human resources department and how that, in turn, affects the activities of the department. Typical human resources functions include:

- Employment and placement
- Wage and salary administration
- Training and development
- Benefits administration
- Outplacement
- Research and information management

Each of the various functions are described in this section.

Employment and Placement

Many new human resources personnel are surprised and a bit disappointed when they realize their department does not make the actual hiring decisions for their organization. For most employers, hiring is done by the department needing staff. That department is best equipped to judge the qualifications of candidates for the job they seek to fill. Human resources departments, however, will often collect applications and résumés, assemble the candidates' files for the department, and perform credential checks and background investigations, as required. Human resources personnel often provide training workshops for supervisors and their staff on how to conduct interviews fairly and objectively and on other aspects of the hiring process. Except in cases of heavy demand for lower-level employees, the human resources department seldom hires anyone except someone for human resources.

After an employee is hired, it often is the responsibility of the human resources department to orient the new employee. This may include an actual tour of the employer's facility and will surely include a discussion of rules and regulations, policies and procedures, benefits, and compensation.

Most organizations publish an employee manual, and it is often provided to the new employee at this initial meeting. This is an exciting time for a new employee and a pleasant interview for the human resources professional. It can represent the many rewarding aspects of employment with this particular employer.

But employers change over time. The marketplace may create new demands; products and services change; and outside economic conditions can create internal changes. Whatever the reason, most organizations are seldom static in terms of staffing needs, and the human resources professional is frequently asked to assess departmental needs for new personnel or to examine an area suspected of having too many workers. To carry out this function, the human resources worker needs to understand the department and the various roles its workers play so he or she can offer effective solutions to staffing situations. Some employees may be transferred, while others face lay-offs or termination. Because personnel costs often represent the largest consistent expense of an organization, the human resources professional's role here is critical to the financial success of the organization.

The psychology major will have little difficulty in bringing psychology studies to bear on the employment and placement activities of the organization. Issues of self-esteem, job definition and structure, and, most important, smooth entry into a new organization are all possible sources of anxiety for a new employee at any level. Your sensitivity to these issues will help you in working with department managers to better define job parameters, plan for dignified and responsible interviewing procedures that give each candidate a fair chance, and arrange for a first-day orientation and tour that says, "Welcome aboard."

Wage and Salary Administration

Basic salaries, opportunities for wage increases, and deductions for various benefits are of crucial importance to all employees. We may not understand everything on our pay stub, but we notice if the total amount goes up or down! After all, pay is described by Abraham Maslow, founder of the humanistic perspective, as a basic need, and it guarantees many of our lower-level needs, such as housing, food, and security. Understanding this, a psychology major will recognize how important it is to educate workers on their pay, how it works, and the reasons for any changes. They'll best appreciate the need to alert employees well in advance of possible change, and to anticipate questions and provide materials that satisfy those questions.

A psychology major in human resources appreciates that many people define their success by their salary level, make comparisons to others of similar employment level, and are on the alert for any discrepancies or hints of discrimination. Wages and salary are a sensitive and complex issue. The psychology major who understands and appreciates those ramifications will become a real asset to the human resources department.

Training and Development

Depending on the number of employees and the size of the human resources department, training and development may be conducted in-house or contracted out to other professionals. In most cases, it is a combination. In-house human resources professionals will offer workshops year-round on issues as diverse as retirement planning, safe driving, employee safety and health precautions, and effective use of employee benefits. There may be workshops on stress management, promotion opportunities, and new supervisor training workshops. Outside professionals may be called in to run cholesterol tests and education programs, as well as multicultural and diversity workshops. Here's an entry-level job advertisement that focuses on training:

Sales Training Specialist. Provide comprehensive, professional, & effective development materials & programs for sales support team; design curriculum materials to be used on Learning Management System; develop & write sales curriculum and field support materials. Required: bachelor's degree, working knowledge of Windows products, ability to prioritize multiple tasks.

Staff training and development is rewarding both in the design and delivery of these training sessions. Workers value good on-the-job training and their feedback will often suggest further areas for enrichment. With issues facing the workplace such as compliance with the Americans with Disabilities Act (ADA), spousal benefits for same-sex partners, and a host of equally complicated issues, staff training and development not only builds a sense of employee cohesion and camaraderie, but it is often a deliberate response to critical issues facing the workplace and its employees.

The psychology major looks out over the range and variety of employees in an organization and realizes that each person is at a different developmental and career stage. Some are young and ambitious, eager for change and growth, and flexible with their time and life. Others are embarking on relationships or starting families and must, for the present time, concentrate their energies on these important life choices. Some may be continuing their education; others may be anticipating slowing down their schedules, working less, and easing into retirement. Each is in a different place in his or her work life, chronological age, personal development, and identification with the organization.

Your appreciation of these differences can spark ideas and strategies for wonderful and varied training and development programs. "Managing a Two-Career Family," "Planning for Retirement," "Stress-Reduction Techniques," and "Flex-Time or Work-at-Home-Scheduling" are just some of the training possibilities. You can help educate a workforce whose need for information about improving their jobs; managing work, careers, and home; and continuing personal development is inexhaustible.

Benefits Administration

No human resources office is open for any length of time before the paperwork involved in benefits administration begins to accumulate. Requests for tuition reimbursement; worker's compensation; dental, medical, and optical care; pension planning; and 401(k)s pile up. The list is ever-changing as each organization offers a unique blend of employee benefits, and the menu also often changes depending upon the status of the employee. Full-time employees receive a full complement of benefits, and those who work less than full time often have their benefits prorated.

It adds up to a mountain of paperwork. While some employees have horror stories of how human resources mismanaged a benefits claim, far more will speak of excellent benefits and thoughtful and caring benefits administrators who are sensitive and discreet in the processing of the ever-present forms.

Benefits administration serves a vital purpose within the organization and must address emerging issues. For example, despite stepped-up drug testing by employers, use of methamphetamines in the workplace is growing rapidly. Many firms understand and deal with the issues of drug and alcohol abuse among their workers, and they have built programs that will refer these employees to off-site employee assistance programs for counseling and treatment. In the majority of cases, these employees continue working or return to full employment following a course of treatment.

Employers realize that the physical and mental health of their employees play a key role in productivity. Whether an organization provides exercise rooms or has a professional making mental health referrals, it knows it will see sharply reduced absenteeism, fewer claims on employee health and benefits programs, and increased productivity because of these efforts. So, while the human resources promotional literature emphasizes enhanced benefits to the employee, the rewards for the employer are savings in dollars and cents.

Benefits administration could be a deeply rewarding job function to the psychology major, especially today as organizations become ever more sensitive to human needs and the relationship between satisfying those needs and work productivity. You can hardly function well at work if you're worried about retirement finances or the hospitalization costs for your child's chronic illness. Psychology majors employed in human resources work will have continuous opportunities to review benefit options and consider new proposals that might directly address your employees' needs.

Outplacement

Most organizations now make provisions for helping their employees' transition out of the organization, regardless of the situation that might precipitate such a move. Even in the case of termination of employment, many employers provide an exit interview to allow the terminated employee an opportunity to express anger or disappointment and to discuss the events and situations surrounding the termination.

When employers downsize their organization to respond to economic or market pressures and employees must be terminated regardless of their performance, more and more firms are providing the services of outplacement firms. These specialty organizations help the terminated workers through counseling, help with résumé writing and interview skills, and job leads. The human resources personnel connect employees with outplacement firms.

But even successful employers don't train managers on how to let an employee go. When managers do have to fire someone, they are apt to do it awkwardly because of their lack of training. Employers often neglect to give their senior staff training in how to approach a termination meeting. In addition, the employer may not have follow-up counseling services in place or realize they do not have all the resources to put together an exemplary outplacement program. If you're a psychology major and thinking, "I see an opportunity to make a difference," you'd be right. Understanding human behavior and appreciating the difficulties of a job-loss situation, the psychology major will look at his or her organization and help build a program that encompasses staff training, sensitivity, follow-up counseling, and a minimum of exposure and embarrassment for the terminated employee.

Research and Information Management

Requests for a history of worker's compensation claims, for average salary increases for middle management, or for any kind of information having to do with employees, their numbers, cost, productivity, and changes over time are directed to the human resources department. The staff needs to be comfortable analyzing and providing data that will be useful to management in making personnel and strategic decisions.

The Americans with Disabilities Act (ADA), contract negotiations and arbitration, Equal Employment Opportunity (EEO) initiatives, fair wage standards, and Occupational Safety and Health Administration (OSHA) guidelines, as well as an organization's own internal grievance process, all require research and information paperwork in addition to the meetings, planning sessions, hearings, and presentations these issues generate.

To be prepared with this kind of information requires excellent record keeping with an eye to data retrieval. This is one of the many reasons why a human resources office is often very concerned about paperwork and administration and why some entry-level employees are disappointed to discover the human resources function is not as social as they had anticipated.

As a psychology major, you're ready for this task because you've not only had to deal with numerous research reports in your studies, but you also have probably created some data yourself and had to transform that data into meaningful information for a paper or class presentation. Human resources work is no different. It might be salary equity among female managers of a certain rank or uniform costs for certain employees. Whatever the informational demands, you should find your major has prepared you well.

Review these three job descriptions for entry-level workers and notice the range of duties required of each.

> **Human Resources Analyst.** [Area water district in NV] seeks candidate to plan & implement employee recruitment & selection activities for assigned job classes; confer with hiring authorities on job demands & appropriate requirements; develop & conduct outreach recruitment programs to obtain qualified candidates; develop job announcements, advertisements, & other material; screen applications for qualifications. Minimum qualifications: graduation from four-year college with major course work in human resources,

continued

psychology, or related field; one year of experience; or equivalent combination of training & experience. Will be required to pass drug screening test & background check and job-related physical evaluation.

Human Resources Assistant. [Sub-prime mortgage company in DE] has exciting opportunity in HR. Duties include: prepare offer request/new hire paperwork; create & maintain employee files; review docs for newly added employees; conduct employment verifications; respond to unemployment claim requests; maintain & distribute performance review notification reports to management; update & maintain turnover reports & organizational chart; draft letters, memos, & reports; assist with events coordination. Requires bachelor's degree; must be skilled in various software applications; must have excellent written/verbal communication, analytical, time management, & teamwork skills; must have ability to work in fast-paced environment. Experience with HR-specific software desirable. Ability to work overtime as needed. Competitive salary & benefits; casual work atmosphere.

Human Resources Coordinator. [Nonprofit in TX] seeks candidate for related processing & data entry; assist with recruitment; administer volunteer process; handle general office duties as needed. Bachelor's degree, strong communications skills.

Training and Qualifications

Having read the information on the functions and working conditions of a human resources department and still feeling strongly that you can bring your psychology education to bear on the work of such an office, you may be wondering, "Do I need experience in human resources to be considered for this type of work?" The answer is that there is much you can do to convince an employer you are ready to work in a human resources position.

The foregoing discussion of human resources functions suggests many of the skills and attributes that will be important to a new human resources professional. But there are others that are important as well.

Communication

In both verbal and written communications, human resources professionals need to be very careful of their language, specifically its accuracy, tone, and nuance. Notice the emphasis on communications skills in the following ads.

Human Resources Representative, [Logistics and transportation company] to serve as a HR generalist. Will resolve employee concerns, provide counsel & guidance to management, coach and assist with training initiatives . . . must have highly developed communications [verbal & written, and interpersona] skills. . . .

Human Resources Generalist. [Mortgage company] helps management support HR initiatives. Participate in workforce recruitment, training, performance management, and employee communication. Must have excellent communications skills [verbal, written and presentation]. . . .

Human Resources Representative. [Marketing firm] will assist leaders with development & execution of annual reviews & compensation plans . . . must have strong interviewing skills and relationship-building ability.

Most of the issues dealt with in human resources departments are critical to employees, and work conditions can be vital to an employee's sense of self-esteem and sense of identity. Change, even the suggestion of change, can provoke great anxiety among some employees, and how such change is presented is crucial to the success of any plan. Your communications skills will be called in to play again.

Let's say your firm has decided to purchase a new telephone system that requires each employee to "key in" their own identification number for every call. Prior to this, phone charges have been lumped by department for each extension number anonymously. The policy has been an unwritten one that reasonable numbers of personal phone calls (calls home, to your spouse, etc.) were okay. Now, with a new caller ID number, many employees will be frightened about the loss of that privilege. Knowing this, you may want to specifically address this issue in your memo and reassure staff members that reasonable personal calls are still allowed.

One-on-one conferences, small group and department meetings, memoranda, and policies and procedures manuals all need to contain clear and direct language so all staff members can understand and carry out human resources initiatives. An early independent project for the psychology major employed in human resources might be to collect and review literature and promotional materials from other public organizations for sensitive and clear language, and then compare it to your own firm's written work. There may be some opportunities to improve your organization's materials through careful editing.

Public Presentation Skills

For efficiency and because many human resources programs affect large groups of employees, you may be frequently presenting material to large groups. Professional staff needs to have excellent public presentation skills, including the ability to plan, organize, and write a workshop or seminar; design and execute effective and appropriate visual materials; and design and execute forms for evaluation. Technical competency with computerized presentations and audiovisual materials, including VCRs, video-recording equipment, and overhead projectors, is certainly a plus.

If you've had experience with presentations and technical aids in college, be sure to feature that on your résumé or in a cover letter. Skilled presenters are always in demand, especially when they are comfortable with a variety of technologies that can be used to improve communication and retention.

Computer and Software Familiarity

As with all administrative units, the use of computers in a human resources department is pervasive. Database management skills are crucial for data analysis and retrieval as are word-processing skills, which are used for employee communications. This job description highlights the skills one employer is seeking:

Human Resources Assistant. (Retail) is looking for a human resources generalist to assist the Director of Human Resources with all aspects of the function. Responsibilities will include recruitment, salary and benefits administration, personnel policies and procedures, and payroll. Qualifications: excellent verbal and written communications skills, computer proficiency using Microsoft Word, Excel, and Filemaker Pro software. Organizational skills, high degree of accuracy, attention to detail, and the ability to maintain confidentiality are essential.

Many departments produce their own brochures and information pieces, and rely on staff who have desktop publishing and Windows software capability. Just as it is a safe assumption that all human resources staff at every level of management and seniority employ some degree of computer use in this exciting and demanding field, it is likewise a safe assumption that the entry-level candidate with strong computer skills stands a markedly increased opportunity for employment than the candidate who is less comfortable using computer technology.

Have you included your computer and data management courses on your résumé? If not, be sure to mention them in your cover letter or during an interview. Reading about human resources, you've become aware of the vast amounts of data and detail that are going to be stored electronically. It's ironic, but true, that to perform your human resources task in a very human, connected manner with your employees, you need to be the very best at utilizing computer technology.

If you have a chance to meet and talk with a human resources professional (perhaps an alumni meeting arranged through your career office alumni connection), ask them about data technology experience. How much did they have coming into the job and how much do they have now? How big a part of their day does computer technology play? Do they have human resources data analysts on staff? Who inputs their data? A discussion about computer technology will help you put a new, and more realistic, face on human resources work.

Data Analysis

Human resources may be about people, but the paper can sure get in the way. To the rather tired statement heard from the young job candidate applying for a human resources position that he or she is "a people person," most hiring professionals might chuckle and say most days they could use a good data analyst. As with so many issues, the reality is somewhere in the middle of those two extremes.

The effective use of and provision for the employment pool in any organization takes inordinate amounts of planning and analysis, and it demands staff comfortable with translating raw data into meaningful information for management to use in decision making.

For every human interaction—one-on-one meeting, public presentation to a department or group of employees, new staff orientation—much time is spent analyzing data concerning staff. Overtime and associated costs, sick days and temporary help expenditures, vacation scheduling and conflicts, and use of benefits all need to be monitored and understood.

The psychology major knows enough not to confuse data with individual human interaction, but data do reveal trends and can indicate problems. Often, these data are warning signs that lead to conferences, meetings, and lots of human interaction as you seek solutions. The psychology major brings an ability to bridge the anonymous, cold data and the real, live human interactions the data represent.

Earnings

The Society for Human Resource Management conducts, in partnership with Mercer Human Resources Consulting, Inc., the Human Resource Management Compensation Survey (shrm.org). Their annual survey contains useful salary information broken down by region, industry, and selected locations. In the table below we show salaries at the 25th percentile of the pay range. We believe these are realistic starting salaries for someone with the type of credentials the psychology major has to offer. Be sure to check with a regional association that can tell you how salaries vary in its area, or check websites that show current salary information by specific job title. One good example is monster.com's salary center.

Region	25th Percentile of Salary
North Central	$38,200
Northeast	$40,300
Southeast	$38,300
South Central	$39,900
West Coast	$43,200

Career Outlook

The number and types of positions in human resources vary dramatically, depending on the size of the organization, the current state of its fiscal health, and the emphasis the organization puts on its employees and their welfare. Human resources is not a revenue-producing department. Unlike the sales force whose high personnel expenses are offset by the generation of income for the firm, the human resources department is pure administration and seen as overhead. Consequently, during difficult times it is often tapped to trim staff or not rehire empty positions, thereby ensuring greater profitability for the organization.

Entry-level positions are best selected from among medium-sized to large-sized organizations, and in those industries and economic sectors that are enjoying current profitability and growth. Demographic analysis indicates that the United States has an aging "baby boom" population that is going to stay in the workforce longer and more effectively than their predecessors. They are expected to enjoy healthier, more active, and longer retirements, suggesting future growth in industries involving financial planning, medical institutions, planned retirement homes and communities, and geriatric services in general.

Strategy for Finding the Jobs

Entry-level human resources positions are filled by graduates who come from a variety of academic disciplines, so expect that the level of competition for these positions will be keen. We suggest focusing on a three-pronged job search strategy. You will want to be sure to build some human resources knowledge and skills into your background (suggestions for doing so are discussed later). In addition, you must be ready to relate how your psychology training has prepared you to work effectively in this field. Both your résumé and your interview comments must highlight the relevance of this training. And, finally, focus on an employment setting that seems like a good fit for you to begin your human resources career.

Build Some Human Resources Knowledge and Skills into Your Background

As you move through your college career, be sure to take courses that relate to human resources and work to gain some actual experience in the field. Often, business departments at colleges offer courses in personnel or human/industrial relations. Minoring in one of these areas would be especially useful, but if that option is not available, take as much related course work as you can. Consider a for-credit internship and get credit and hands-on experience at the same time.

In addition to your academic preparation, you'll want to explore two areas:

1. Deepening your understanding of the current societal trends that affect the functions and mission of a human resources department
2. Becoming more knowledgeable about the legal issues the human resources professional faces

Deepen Your Understanding of Current Societal Trends. The discussion in this chapter offers a basic explanation of human resources, but the related functions vary dramatically by organization, product or service, and even geographic region. For example, many of our newer, cutting-edge technological firms have instituted some of the newest and often most controversial employee benefit programs. Many have proven comfortable with work-at-home personnel, flex-time, and very loose organizational structures. Such policies might not succeed in a more traditional organization with a less-sophisticated or less-educated employment pool. Current news sources will often feature stories on various industries and a continued awareness of these stories will help you to become conversant with trends that affect the current state of human resources administration.

Become More Knowledgeable About Legal Issues. To prepare yourself for seeking positions in this field, become more knowledgeable about the legal issues as well as the issues with legal implications that increasingly dominate this field. Reading current literature will suggest many of these topics. More focused reading materials can be found online, in your local or university library, or at your career office. The Society for Human Resource Management's *HR Magazine* and the American Society for Training and Development's *Training and Development Journal* are two good examples. Both are available in paper or electronic format. Some of the topics you'll want to be familiar with include:

- Safety and health
- Employment and staffing
- Employment law
- Compensation
- Benefits
- Technology

You do not need to become an expert on these topics, but they are important issues to human resources professionals. Your job search will be far more successful if you can demonstrate a competent awareness and appreciation for the challenges of these areas. In many cases, your knowledge of legal issues will overcome any hesitancy an employer may feel for your lack of direct experience. Your willingness to self-educate is, in and of itself, a strong employment consideration.

Use your summers or periods of part-time employment to find out as much as you can about working in human resources. If you are not employed in that department, network with the director or manager of personnel to let them know about your interests and to see if they can assist you in getting information or making contacts in the field. You may want to invest in joining a professional personnel or human resources organization (see the list at the end of this chapter) to continue your networking and to begin hearing about actual employment opportunities.

Relate Your Psychology Training on the Résumé and in the Interview

Your psychology degree has helped you develop many skills important to working effectively in human resources (communications skills, public presentation skills, computer and software familiarity, data analysis). But your skills and knowledge may not be readily apparent to a potential employer. Don't let them guess about how well qualified you are; show them on your résumé and in your interview. Point out your relevant training and tell him or her how you can help accomplish the company's human resources goals.

Focus on an Employment Setting That Seems Like a Good Fit for You

In the next section, a wide range of employers is described. You may be able to picture yourself working in some settings and also know immediately that you wouldn't feel comfortable in others. Review the section, and make a decision about where you would like to begin your employment search. You may have to widen the scope of your search, depending on the geographic area where you live and the types of employers you decide to focus on first. But start with an industry that looks like the best fit.

Possible Employers

Personnel, training, and labor-relations specialists and managers are found in every industry, from manufacturing to banking, from transportation to health care. We will begin acquainting you with some of the possibilities in the descriptions provided in this section, which include:

Health care
Service
Education
Manufacturing
Finance and insurance
Government
Staffing companies

Your job search should begin with a review of all types of possible employers. After you have familiarized yourself with the range of possibilities, begin your job search by starting to network with professionals and then apply for jobs in two or three industries.

Health Care

Health-care facilities employ doctors, nurses, technicians, food-service workers, maintenance workers, administrators, managed-care coordinators, social workers, and a host of other types of employees. The human resources professional can play a critical role in filling positions with the right people.

Help in Locating These Employers. Several good resources are *Career Opportunities in Health Care*, the *Encyclopedia of Medical Organizations and Agencies* (check your library for this one), and the Medical and Health Care Jobs website (nationjob.com/medical). Be sure to directly contact those health organizations you would like to work for, and do some informational interviewing or inquire about how they advertise job openings.

Service

No matter where you go, whether it's in food retailing, household furniture and appliance sales, clothing sales, travel services, or business and professional services, personnel are available to assist you. Medium-sized and large-sized organizations have human resources professionals who help them hire people who are willing to work to support organizational goals and serve customers.

Help in Locating These Employers. Because the service industry is so large, we will present just a few resources that will be useful in your job search. Be sure to ask for recommendations from the other professionals you are working with, career counselors, and librarians. Depending on your interests, you may want to review Yahoo's website for the various industries (yahoo.com), usabanks.org for a list of banks by state, *Standard Directory of Advertising Agencies*, *O'Dwyer's Directory of Public Relations Firms*, *Ward's Business Directory of U.S. Private and Public Companies* (at your library), and *Hoover's Handbook of American Business*.

Education

Higher-education employers, including community, two-year, and four-year colleges, hire a variety of workers to help them achieve their educational mission and goals. Whether it is the custodian who keeps the facility in shape, the teacher in the classroom, the support or technical staff member, or the administrator, all are important, and the human resources worker helps find the right person for the right job.

Help in Locating These Employers. Resources that will be useful in identifying schools that have a need for human resources personnel include three of Peterson's (petersons.com) references: *Guide to Two-Year Colleges*, *Guide to Four-Year Colleges*, and *Guides to Graduate Study*. Peterson's website can also link you to the website of many, many educational institutions where HR positions would be listed. *The Chronicle of Higher Education's* website (chronicle.com) also contains job listings for you to review.

Manufacturing

Whether a company is manufacturing broad woven fabric, hats and gloves, wood office furniture, folding cardboard boxes, tires, abrasive products, farm machinery, sewing machines, automobiles, or costume jewelry, there are human resources personnel who have screened, processed, oriented, trained, and provided benefits to the labor force. As America fights to maintain its competitiveness in manufacturing, it needs competent human resources workers to assemble a well-qualified group of employees.

Help in Locating These Employers. One way to begin locating manufacturing firms is to enter the term "manufacturers association" in your favorite search engine. You'll see listings for hardwood, toy, chemical, and apparel manufacturers associations, just to name a few. Click on a type of association and you will find a list of members. Voila! You have a list to explore. You'll want to become familiar with the Standard Industrial Coding (SIC) scheme, which groups manufacturers producing similar products, to find environments in which you are interested in working. Also, contact your local chamber of commerce for assistance in identifying manufacturing firms operating in your area.

Finance and Insurance

The finance and insurance industry includes commercial banks, savings institutions, and insurance companies. The psychology major can bring personal interest, general knowledge, and relevant skills, such as personal computer and software usage, to this sector of the economy.

Help in Locating These Employers. If you would like to begin generating a list of possible employment sites, begin by visiting websites such as bankjobs.com, banking.com, or A.M. Best Company's ambest.com. They connect you with industry news, employers, and associations. You may also find that companies in this industry recruit on your campus—check with your career services office for a listing. And don't forget to check the yellow pages (online or in print) for organizations doing business in your area.

Federal Government

The federal government competes with the private sector for well-educated, trained workers, including personnel managers. To attract more candidates, the government has made sweeping changes in how it provides information about the offices and agencies that carry out the federal government's charges and also in how it advertises job vacancies. The Office of Personnel Management (OPM) is the federal government's human resources agency. They ensure that the nation's civil service remains free of political influence and that federal employees are selected on the basis of merit and are treated fairly. The OPM maintains regional offices and a website (opm.gov) to assist potential and current employees. A list of OPM sites is included at the end of this chapter.

Some agencies, such as the Central Intelligence Agency, Federal Bureau of Investigation, Defense Intelligence Agency, and National Security Agency, are not required to hire employees through the OPM. They maintain websites that include their own job listings. Be sure to investigate each agency and find out what the current needs are for personnel managers.

Help in Locating These Employers. Given the ease and availability of accessing the Internet, nearly every federal job is listed on the Web. A good place to start looking for actual job listings is on the OPM's website (usajobs.opm.gov), which explains the federal employment process, lets you look at current job openings, provides general information on federal agencies, and allows you to submit an online application.

If you select the option Current Job Openings and then choose a job category search, one of the options is Human Resources. Select this option and search for all jobs; a list will appear on your screen. Or, enter the keywords "entry-level human resources." Select any of the entries and a detailed job description is provided, including information on whom to contact for more information and how to apply for the specific positions.

State and Local Government

State and larger local governments offer human resources positions that help in staffing departments, including corrections, court systems, education, fire protection, health, highway and street construction, housing and community development, hospitals, libraries, natural resources, police, parks and recreation, sanitation, transportation, utilities, and welfare and human services. Your background in psychology has helped prepare you to process, test, and screen applicants who will then be interviewed by the various departments.

Help in Locating These Employers. Begin your search on the Web. Use your favorite search engine and enter "state of (put state name here)." Once you have navigated to the state's official website, you will find references to state departments. Look for headings such as Employment, Personnel, or Human Resources; then look for job listings. Many states update their listings on a weekly basis. You will also find application procedures and contact names, and most sites will allow you to apply online. Printed resources such as *Opportunities in Government Careers* or *Government Job Finder: Where the Jobs Are in Local, State, and Federal Government* detail ways to work these government systems.

Staffing Companies

The importance of the role that staffing companies play in the workplace continues to grow. According to the American Staffing Association's Staff-Stats (staffingtoday.net/staffstats), U.S. staffing firms employed an average of 2.6 million temporary and contract workers per day. Rather than hiring a regular employee, many organizations will hire a field staffer (temporary employee) to "try out." If all goes well, the staffer may be offered regular employment.

The companies that fill these field-staffing positions need professionals, including graduates with psychology degrees, on their own staffs. A psychology graduate might start out as a service coordinator and be responsible for interviewing and orienting applicants, testing them, making a decision as to whether the agency wants to work with them, evaluating job orders, locating and referring qualified applicants, and writing job advertisements. In this industry the service coordinator can move on to positions in sales, marketing, and management after they have paid their dues as a service coordinator.

Help in Locating These Employers. An easy way to begin locating staffing companies is to visit the American Staffing Association's website (staffing today.net/jobseek), enter some key information, and then see a list of companies in that geographic area. Or, review the yellow pages for the geographic area where you would like to work. Search under Employment Agencies,

Employment Contractors–Temporary Help, and Employment Service–Employee Leasing. You will probably be surprised at the number of agencies listed.

Possible Job Titles

Because human resources workers can be generalists or specialists, depending on the size and complexity of the organization, you will see quite a range of job titles. Consider them all when deciding which positions you're qualified to fill or determining an area in which you would like to specialize.

Affirmative-action coordinator
Arbitrator
Benefits adjuster
Benefits administrator
Benefits analyst
Benefits manager
Compensation specialist
Curriculum development specialist
Education specialist
Employee development specialist
Employee relations representative
Employee welfare officer/manager
Employer relations representative
Employment interviewer
Employment specialist
Equal Employment Opportunity (EEO) representative
Grievance officer
Human resources analyst
Human resources assistant
Human resources coordinator
Human resources generalist
Human resources information systems specialist
Human resources representative
Human resources specialist
Industrial relations specialist
Interviewer
Job analyst

Job classification specialist
Labor relations specialist
Management analyst
Mediator
Occupational analyst
Personnel administrator
Personnel consultant
Personnel director
Personnel management specialist
Personnel officer
Personnel staffing specialist
Position classification specialist
Position classifier
Position review specialist
Recreation specialist
Recruiter
Sales training specialist
Service coordinator
Staffing coordinator
Test development specialist
Trainer
Training specialist

Related Occupations

Some attributes of successful human resources workers include the ability to communicate successfully in interactions with other people, attend to details in completing necessary paperwork, and accurately implement and use appropriate assessment instruments. Other professions that require the use of at least some of these same attributes include:

Career planning and placement counselor
Education administrators
Executive assistant (nonprofit organization)
Labor relations manager
Lawyer
Operations manager
Psychologist

Public relations specialist
Rehabilitation counselor
Social worker
Sociologist
Teacher

Many other job titles could be added to this list. As you undertake your exploration, be sure to consider and find out about other job titles you encounter.

Professional Associations

If you are interested in pursuing a career in human resources, several associations serve this group of workers. Review the listings that follow and decide whether any of the groups can provide information relevant to your job search.

American Arbitration Association
335 Madison Ave., 10th Floor
New York, NY 10017-4605
adr.org
Members/Purpose: Helps to resolve a wide range of disputes through mediation, arbitration, elections, and other out-of-court settlement procedures
Training: Conducts workshops, seminars, conferences, and skill-building sessions
Journals/Publications: *Dispute Resolution Journal, Dispute Resolution Times,* ADRWorld.com, *ADR & the Law, Labor Arbitration: What You Need to Know, On and Off the Record: Colosi on Negotiation*
Job Listings: Regional offices sometimes have listings; office locations listed on the website

American Society for Healthcare Human Resources Administration
c/o American Hospital Association
One N. Franklin
Chicago, IL 60606
ashhra.org
Members/Purpose: To provide effective and continuous leadership in the field of health-care human resources administration

Journals/Publications: *Human Resources Administrator*; directory of consultants
Job Listings: Job Networks link on website

American Society for Training and Development
1640 King St.
Box 1443
Alexandria, VA 22313
astd.org
Members/Purpose: Dedicated to workplace learning and performance professionals, with members in multinational corporations, medium-sized and small businesses, government, academia, consulting firms, and product and service suppliers
Training: Provides information on conferences and training programs
Journals/Publications: *Training and Development Journal*, Make Training Evaluation Work, Communication Skills Training, Performance Basics, *T&D Magazine, Learning Circuits* newsletter
Job Listings: Hosts an online job bank

American Staffing Association
277 S. Washington St., Suite 200
Alexandria, VA 22314
staffingtoday.net
Members/Purpose: Promotes the interests of the industry through legal and legislative advocacy, public relations, education, and the establishment of high standards of ethical conduct; ensures the quality of temporary help services and promotes flexible employment opportunities
Job Listings: Online link to Job Seek

College and University Professional Association for Human Resources
2607 Kingston Pike, Suite 250
Knoxville, TN 37919
cupa.org
Members/Purpose: Serves more than 6,500 human resources administrators at nearly 1,600 colleges and universities as well as others interested in the advancement of human resources in higher education
Training: Offers many professional development opportunities
Journals/Publications: CUPA-HR News, CUPA-HR Journal; directory
Job Listings: Website has link to Jobline

International Association of Workforce Professionals
1801 Louisville Rd.
Frankfort, KY 40601
iawponline.org
Members/Purpose: Develop, serve, and support those interested in
workforce development programs
Training: Offers many education and training opportunities
Journals/Publications: *Workforce Professional* newsletter

**International Foundation of Employee
Benefit Plans**
18700 W. Bluemound Rd.
P.O. Box 69
Brookfield, WI 53008-0069
ifebp.org
Members/Purpose: Serves the employee benefits and compensation
industry, with thirty-five thousand individual members representing
8,500 multiemployer trust funds, corporations, public employee groups,
and professional advisory firms throughout the United States and
Canada
Training: Offers a broad selection of conferences and training for
professional growth
Journals/Publications: *Legal-Legislative Reporter* monthly newsletter;
Benefits & Compensation Digest monthly publication
Job Listings: Website contains link to job listings

**International Public Management Association for
Human Resources**
1617 Duke St.
Alexandria, VA 22314
ipma-hr.org
Members/Purpose: Represents the interests of more than 7,500 human
resource professionals at the federal, state, and local levels of
government. Members consist of all levels of public sector HR
professionals. Goal is to provide information and assistance to help HR
professionals increase their job performance and overall agency function
Training: Offers training and certification programs
Journals/Publications: *IPMA-HR News* monthly publications; *Public
Personnel Management* quarterly publication
Job Listings: Website links to monster.com's related jobs

National Association of Personnel Services
The Village at Banner Elk, Suite 108
P.O. Box 2128
Banner Elk, NC 28604
recruitinglife.com
Members/Purpose: Represents profession in critical legislative arenas in
Washington, D.C.; provides legislative guidance and aid in states where
government affairs challenges exist; creates a structure of ethical
practices for industry self-regulation; increases public & business
awareness of the value of personnel services; and educates members &
nonmembers toward better practices and the maintenance of high
professional standards
Training: Conducts certification program and offers a variety of
professional development workshops
Journals/Publications: *Inside NAPS* newsletter; membership directory

National Association of State Personnel Executives
c/o Council of State Governments
2760 Research Park Dr.
P.O. Box 11910
Lexington, KY 40578-1910
naspe.net
Members/Purpose: To enhance communication and the exchange of
information among personnel executives; membership comprised of the
chief personnel executive and their chief deputy or designee from each
of the United States, the Territories of Guam, the Virgin Islands,
American Samoa, the Northern Mariana Islands, the Commonwealth of
Puerto Rico, and the District of Columbia
Journals/Publications: *Inside NASPE* monthly e-newsletter; NASPE
E-xecutive weekly electronic newsletter

Society for Human Resources Management
1800 Duke St.
Alexandria, VA 22314-1997
shrm.org
Members/Purpose: Serves the needs of HR professionals by providing
essential and comprehensive resources
Training: Offers educational opportunities and conferences
Journals/Publications: *HR Magazine*; *HR News*
Job Listings: See HR Careers link on website

WorldatWork
14040 N. Northsight Blvd.
Scottsdale, AZ 85260
worldatwork.org
Members/Purpose: Managerial and professional-level administrative personnel in business, industry, and government responsible for the establishment, execution, administration, or application of compensation practices and policies in their organizations
Training: Annual conference, local group events, and Webinars
Journals/Publications: *WorldatWork* journal, *workspan* magazine, *Canadian News*, *ACA Journal*
Job Listings: JobLinks page on website

Excepted Federal Agencies

Excepted service agencies set their own qualification requirements and are not subject to the appointment, pay, and classification rules that most federal agencies are, by law, required to follow. However, they are subject to veterans' preference. Some federal agencies, for example, the Federal Bureau of Investigation (FBI) and the Central Intelligence Agency (CIA) have only excepted service positions. In other instances, certain organizations within an agency, or even specific jobs may be excepted from civil service procedures. Positions may be in the excepted service by law, executive order, or action of OPM.

Following is a partial list of federal agencies, bureaus, and departments you may want to contact:

Agency for International Development
2401 E St. NW, Room 1127
Washington, DC 20523
usaid.gov

Central Intelligence Agency
Office of Personnel
Washington, DC 20505
cia.gov

Defense Intelligence Agency
Civilian Personnel Office DAH-2
100 MacDill Blvd.
Washington, DC 20340-5100
dia.mil

**Department of Veterans Affairs, Veterans Health
Administration**
U.S. Department of Veterans Affairs
810 Vermont Ave. NW
Washington, DC 20420
va.gov

Federal Bureau of Investigation
JEH Building, Room 6647
10th St. & Pennsylvania Ave. NW
Washington, DC 20571
fbi.gov

Federal Reserve System, Board of Governors
20th & C St. NW
Washington, DC 20551
federalreserve.gov

General Accounting Office
441 G St. NW, Room 1157
Washington, DC 20548
gao.gov

National Security Agency
College Relations Branch
Fort Meade, MD 20750
nsa.gov

Postal Rates Commission
Administrative Office, Suite 300
Washington, DC 20268-0001
prc.gov

Postal Service
Contact your local Postmaster, usps.gov.

Tennessee Valley Authority
Knoxville Office Complex
400 W. Summit Hill Dr.
Knoxville, TN 37902
tva.gov

U.S. Department of State
Foreign Service Positions, Recruitment Division
P.O. Box 9317, Rosslyn Station
Arlington, VA 22219
state.gov

United States Mission to the United Nations
799 United Nations Plaza
New York, NY 10017
un.int/usa

U.S. Nuclear Regulatory Commission
Division of Organization of Personnel
Resources and Employment Program Branch
Washington, DC 20555
nrc.gov

Judicial Branch

The judicial branch of the federal government includes all legal entities except the U.S. Claims Court. For employment information, contact:

Administrative Office of the U.S. Courts
One Columbus Circle NE, Suite G-200
Washington, DC 20544
uscourts.gov

United States Claims Court
717 Madison Place NW
Washington, DC 20005
uscfc.uscourts.gov

United States Supreme Court Building
Personnel Office
1 First St. NE
Washington, DC 20543

Legislative Branch

The legislative branch of the federal government includes offices of senators and representatives, the Library of Congress, and the U.S. Capitol. For employment information, contact:

Library of Congress
Employment Office
Room 107, Madison Building
Washington, DC 20540
loc.gov

U.S. House of Representatives
House Placement Office
House Office Building,
    Annex 2, Room 219
Third & D St. SW
Washington, DC 20515-6609
house.gov

U.S. Senate
Senate Placement Office
Senate Hart Building,
    Room 142B
Washington, DC 20510
senate.gov

Public International Organizations

The United States holds membership in numerous international organizations that are not part of the federal government. For employment information and application procedures, contact:

International Monetary Fund
Recruiting and Training Div.
700 19th St. NW
Washington, DC 20431
imf.org

Pan American Health Organization
Pan American Sanitary Bureau
Regional Office of the World Health Organization
525 23rd St. NW
Washington, DC 20037
paho.org

United Nations Children's Fund
3 United Nations Plaza
New York, NY 10017
unicef.org

United Nations Development Program
1 United Nations Plaza
New York, NY 10017
undp.org

United Nations Institute for Training and Research
801 United Nations Plaza
New York, NY 10017
unitar.org

United Nations Population Fund
220 E. 42nd St.
New York, NY 10017
unfpa.org

United Nations Secretariat
Office of Personnel Services
Recruitment Programs Section
New York, NY 10017
un.org/documents/st.htm

World Bank, International Finance Corporation and Multilateral Investment Guarantee Agency
Recruitment Div.
International Recruitment
1818 H St. NW
Washington, DC 20433
worldbank.org

9

Path 4: Therapy

The field of psychology is diverse, with emphases ranging from clinical psychology to counseling psychology, developmental psychology to experimental psychology, and school psychology to social psychology. Each one of these subfields is, however, concerned with two things: behavior and the data, facts, and observations relating to that behavior. Undergraduate psychology programs often focus on introducing the student to the full spectrum of behavioral fields, rather than on training the student to work in one particular subfield. Psychology departments are in the business of exposing and exploring the field of psychology and what the study of the human mind and human behavior represents as an academic discipline. They do not train students to diagnose symptoms of pathology and then treat them. Graduate programs in psychology provide this more specific training.

Your undergraduate psychology degree program presented you with texts, readings to digest, and papers to write that allowed you to explore facets of many subfields of psychology. You may also have had an opportunity to do behavior experiments with rodents or other animals. Perhaps, throughout your years of study, many interesting guest speakers visited your campus to talk on human behavior topics. Sometimes, an ambitious student or group of learners, with faculty supervision, will create a survey or conduct an experiment with a consenting group of fellow students on some behavioral topic, such as test anxiety or stress.

Some students gain exposure to working with clients through counseling classes or developmental and industrial psychology courses. Others observe young children or work with residents of nursing homes, patients in hospitals, or workers in factories and corporations. Some academic programs require internships or fellowships in a counseling and psychological-services center or career-counseling office, where students observe the counseling process in both individual and group settings.

Your academic, observational, and/or clinical training has awakened your interest in working in a therapeutic setting, and you're eager to learn more about what types of jobs await you in the world beyond college.

Who Are Therapists?

The group of occupations that we label as therapists are those defined as working to treat and rehabilitate individuals who may present problems that are emotional, mental, or physical. The therapist works with a client to restore and develop function, to prevent the loss of capabilities, and to maintain an optimum lifestyle. An increasing number of therapy modalities, or mediums of therapy, are currently available to patients: exercise, massage, counseling, music, heat, light, aroma, water, electricity, dance, ceramics, and voice are all employed in helping the client regain what has been lost, emotionally, mentally, or physically. These practitioners often work in or close to medically related institutions or programs where the therapy request originates. They are most often part of a larger team of helping professionals who rely on each other for diagnosis and treatment updates. Some of the more frequently encountered therapies are reviewed here.

• **Behavioral therapy.** Behavioral therapy focuses on recognizing and changing specific behavioral patterns. You may have read of its use in treating sexual dysfunctions, specific phobias, or anxiety states (such as a lawyer afraid to talk in court) as well as obsessive-compulsive symptoms. It may be used in conjunction with medication.

• **Cognitive therapy.** Cognitive therapy focuses on recognizing and changing ingrained patterns of negative thinking or assumptions that are negative or counterproductive. It is a treatment modality often used to treat anxiety, specific phobias, drug and alcohol abuse, and mild to moderate depression. Cognitive therapy is sometimes combined with behavioral therapy.

• **Interpersonal therapy.** Interpersonal problems or other relationship difficulties involving people with moderate depression is the focus of interpersonal therapy. It helps a patient identify and modify interpersonal relationships so that the patient feels better about himself or herself.

- **Psychodynamic therapy.** Dealing with deeply ingrained internal emotional struggles and conflicts usually related to early childhood traumas and losses that continue to impair work productivity and personal relationships is the focus of psychodynamic therapy.
- **Family and couples therapy.** Family or couples therapy deals with difficulties within the family or a couple's relationship, focusing on the interpersonal dynamics of the group or unit. This type of therapy involves discussions to solve problems, and the goal is to strengthen communications within the family.
- **Expressive therapy.** Expressive therapy involves the use of creative arts, such as drama, art, music, movement, dance, or poetry. Expressive therapies (each of the expressive arts can be a therapy unto itself) are used in the treatment of a variety of populations (adults with chronic mental illnesses, sexual abuse survivors, youths at risk), in one-on-one sessions and group treatment. There are practitioners labeled expressive therapists, as well as therapists in each of the expressive areas, for example, music therapists, art therapists, and dance therapists.

Where the Psychology Major Fits into the Therapy Picture

At this point in the discussion, the undergraduate with a general psychology degree and an interest in working directly with clients might well ask, "Where could I possibly fit into this employment picture? I am interested in client contact and many of these modalities hold interest for me. But, I only have my bachelor's degree and am not yet ready to pursue additional education." The answer is interesting.

Psychology undergraduates are hired for some preprofessional therapist positions. They are not therapists, in the strict definition of that term, although many job specifications and advertisements will use that title. The positions cover a wide range of duties and responsibilities. The American Psychological Association (apa.org), the preeminent professional group for psychology careerists in the United States, continually surveys the employment of preprofessionals in the area of therapy. They continue to find the overwhelming majority of these entry-level therapy positions to be working with the severely emotionally disturbed. Other large populations receiving therapeutic services from individuals with undergraduate psychology degrees include the neurologically impaired and those who have mental retardation. Consider these advertisements:

Recreation Therapist. (Veterans Affairs Medical Center) plans & conducts therapeutic RT activities for patients on all nursing home units, including geriatric evaluation medical unit, regular units, & respite patients. Develop, coordinate, schedule, & implement RT & weekend leisure program. Develop treatment goals & treatment plans. Participate in quality assurance—collect & analyze data on patient participation & staff productivity. Participate in meetings, in-services, continuing ed., etc. Degree in recreational therapy or a major in an appropriate subject with therapeutic experience. Knowledge of human behavior, psychology, anatomy, & human performance.

Creative Arts Therapist. (Health-care system) conduct evals & plan treatment activities for patients with psychosocial dysfunctions. All work performance to conform to written established hospital policies & procedures & in a manner demonstrating concern & consideration. B.S. degree required with some experience.

After careful consideration, much discussion with professionals in the field, and a survey of job postings available to those with a bachelor's degree in psychology, we have chosen to include therapist positions as one of the five career paths in this book. You will encounter the job title frequently in your job search. Before you make a job choice, we want to help you understand exactly what these positions entail, both the rich rewards and the very heavy responsibilities. To sum up:

1. Therapy positions are advertised and do exist for graduates with a degree in psychology.
2. The people who hold these positions are referred to as therapists but are more accurately described as preprofessionals working under the supervision of a therapist.
3. Preprofessionals do work with patients.
4. Preprofessionals do participate in a variety of therapeutic modalities or treatment plans.
5. All of this work is done under the close supervision of a degreed, trained, and licensed, certified, or registered therapist, and that

therapist is probably part of an even larger care team headed by one or more medical doctors.

Definition of the Career Path

Securing and beginning your psychology career in a therapist position will be a challenge in and of itself. Fortunately, because the work is so rewarding, the effort is well worth it. The daily contact with clients and treatment interventions (activities) will help you build a history of experiences that you will draw from for the rest of your life. If you do begin your career in a therapy position, it is no exaggeration to suggest this will be a determining influence on your psychology career.

However, challenges for baccalaureate-degreed therapists will continue to present themselves, especially in the form of credentials, certification, and training issues. The therapeutic field is one that is under continuous scrutiny from the public, the government, insurers, caregivers, the support networks of the clients, and even its own professional organizations, which are seeking to enhance the credibility and prestige of their profession. Questions of licensure by state officials and certification programs by professional organizations provide a continuous dialogue in the popular press and in professional journals on ethics, standards, educational requirements, and professional criteria for all these therapies.

Professionally, we are witnessing an increased awareness by both the public and the court system of issues surrounding the implicit legal and ethical contract between patient and therapist. For therapists, there are generally four elements to obtaining informed consent from their client: (1) client competency, (2) the disclosure of material information (does the client fully understand the treatment regimen), (3) the client's understanding of the presented material, and (4) voluntary consent.

In addition to attaining an advanced degree as an outward mark of professionalism, many states have both licensure and certification regulations. Licensure has to do with the state ensuring certain educational and experiential standards have been met. It often involves some type of written examination, and it helps the public know that the individual has met some state-mandated criterion for professionalism. Licensing boards are then able to discipline unethical or fraudulent practitioners by revoking this license.

Certification through professional organizations promotes standards of education, practice, accountability, discretion, ethics, and visibility. Certifications help assure the public that the individual therapist has met some established standards. Certification can involve testing or the documentation of professional development and years of practice. It is often issued for a limited period of time. See your state officials for information on licensure and your applicable professional associations for certification information.

Consequently, the impetus is constantly on you to enhance your training, certification, and qualifications for the work that you do. If you find yourself fortunate enough to begin your career in a therapist position, you will want to take every opportunity your employer can provide or that you can afford personally to enhance your training and skill package. Discover what local or state government agencies or professional associations offer in the form of workshops, seminars, and qualifying programs that will add to your professionalism and enhance your value to your employer.

An Example: Expressive Therapy

Perhaps you are interested in an entry-level position as an expressive or art therapist. Art, music, and dance are some of the major therapeutic avenues in what is termed expressive therapy. Generally, these modalities try to involve the client in creative, nonverbal (although there is vocal expressive therapy) expression to help with maladaptive behavior. Take a look at the following advertisements:

Expressive Therapist. Qualified candidate must possess a bachelor's degree in a related field. Must have internship in a psych setting. Must be Certified Therapeutic Recreation Specialist or be CTRS eligible.

Expressive/Recreational Therapist. Children's Hospital, unit for children with PDD, autism, Asperger's, and developmental delays. Looking for an expressive or recreational therapist for Saturday, Sunday, and one day during the week.

Expressive Therapist. Residence & day program for adults with severe & persistent mental illness (mostly psychosis). Carry caseload of five to six clients, run groups, & do tasks related to direct care. Very open to expressive therapy—have music room & art studio.

The expressive therapist is almost always grounded in one medium. The therapist may be a ceramist, modern dancer, or collage artist, and he or she believes strongly in the therapeutic qualities of that form and medium. It has been a salient and critical feature of these therapists' own mental health. It ennobles them, lifts them up, and allows them to express themselves in a way they cannot otherwise. This belief in and personal grounding in the medium for their own self-improvement and revitalization is critical before they can use the therapeutic technique to help others. Incorporating your preferred medium with other possible creatively expressive approaches, you seek to help clients reach this same goal.

Art and expressive therapists are found in many clinical, educational, and rehabilitative settings, although their operating titles may vary. For a number of reasons, including medical school training, individual attending physician exposure, and some generational issues, the expressive therapies may not yet be among the modalities of first choice. The boundaries of this field and the research data to support it are not yet clearly defined.

There is strong support available for expressive therapists that can be found in the training, graduate programs, and established certification standards. Music therapists, for example, may apply for registration with the American Music Therapy Association (musictherapy.org). Qualified music therapists may become board-certified upon passing an exam given by the Certification Board for Music Therapists, an independent accreditation organization. Neither registration nor certification is required at the current time for music therapists to practice, incidentally.

Because most expressive therapists participate with other kinds of therapy treatments (occupational, recreational, and physical therapists) in a team approach for their clients and in institutional settings, they are covered by third-party insurance payments. As an individual, isolated therapy, even under referral by a physician, the patient may find that this therapy is not reimbursable by insurance providers.

Working Conditions

Every therapy is different, every setting in which therapy is practiced is different, and every client is, of course, unique. Can we make any generalizations about your possible working conditions as an entry-level therapist preprofessional? Yes!

Let's begin with clients, because your work begins with them. At any time in your practice, you are apt to have a roster of individual clients. Because you're working in one type of therapy, these clients may share, in a general way, some presenting issues (relationship difficulties, eating disorders, compulsive behaviors) but age, gender, and personality are all different. You'll have clients about to finish their course of therapy, either because of improvement or lack of benefits or finances. You'll have some clients right in the middle of their course of treatment and others just beginning to work with you on their issues. You're in a different place with each client, and as you move from appointment to appointment, you'll consciously have to shift gears and reassess your next appointment. Who are they and where are they in their treatment plan and what is your next step?

To answer these questions, you'll consult two sources: your own process notes that you'll keep on your clients detailing what happened during your previous session and your thoughts and ideas for future sessions. You'll include any "homework" you gave your client for your next appointment and the overall treatment plans for this client. You'll be directed in your efforts by the professionals on your team assigned to supervise and direct your work. As a preprofessional, you'll be supervised quite closely, in most instances, until you have established a track record of trust, responsibility, and performance.

You'll be working to earn your client's trust and acceptance so that you can work with him or her in a productive manner and fulfill the protocols established for his or her therapy. You'll keep notes on your progress, and some of your sessions may be observed or even videotaped. You will be asked to contribute to evaluative reports on clients and documentation surrounding treatment plans for insurance purposes. You may also be asked to help write up case studies for research or publication purposes.

A number of elements of the therapist's working situation, such as teamwork and family involvement, are discussed next.

Teamwork

The hallmark of the therapist's job is teamwork. Consulting with other preprofessionals and professionals to ensure the most considerate implementation of the treatment plan for the client can be complicated with many intervening variables. If you are working with a recovering adolescent drug abuser who also happens to be profoundly deaf and whose speech is difficult to interpret, you may find yourself working closely with a speech therapist. Combinations and recombinations of team members are the rule, not the exception, and each member of the team is expected to maintain excellent communication, positive and energetic commitment to the client, superb and detailed record keeping, and a respect for scheduled appointments.

Group Settings

Oftentimes, because many clients share similar issues (early sexual abuse, eating disorders, or nonspecific anxiety), using the therapy in a group setting is appropriate and beneficial. Conducting group psychotherapy is a special skill that has many transferable applications to other employment settings, and if you are able to learn and observe some group counseling techniques (building cohesion, norming, consensual validation), you would be well-advised to take every advantage of the opportunity. You will draw upon that experience throughout your work life in almost any setting involving teams.

Family Involvement

Families often become involved in the therapy of one of their members. It may be a young boy acting out over his parents' divorce or an elderly patient who has become despondent about the death of a spouse. There will be consultations with the family about home life, and there may be instructions to avoid certain behaviors or situations that are problematical for the client. Occasionally, family members may be asked to participate in the therapy.

Supervision

In all cases where preprofessionals engage in many of the same treatment modalities as professionals, they are under the supervision of those more qualified and do not function with as much autonomy. Even as you establish a track record of performance and successful interventions with patients, you will be given very little freedom. This supervision protects the client and the professional from charges of malfeasance, mismanagement, and unethical behavior. If this supervision becomes too confining for you, it may be an excellent signal that the time has come for you to consider becoming a degreed therapist in your own right.

Length of Treatment

Therapists engage in both short-term and long-term treatment interventions. How long your clients stay in therapy may be important to you because it affects your interaction with them. At the extreme ends of the spectrum, in short-term therapy, you will have a constantly changing population of clients seeing you for a limited number of sessions (often less than five). Short-term therapy has many proponents, including third-party insurers, and for some presenting issues, it can be effective. The pace may be rapid with much client diversity, and so there may be little closure.

Long-term therapy allows you to work intensively with clients and mark progress over time. Therapeutic options increase with the number of sessions as do the options for connection with your clients. On the other hand, many psychoanalysts (who may see their patients several times a week) will tell you there can be a corresponding static quality, with little dramatic change day-to-day and a numbing predictability.

Training and Qualifications

Several training and qualifications issues are extremely important for the therapist. They include possession of advanced degrees, licensure and certification, work experience, and certain personal qualifications.

Advanced Degrees

There is no question that the predominance of therapist positions begin with a demand for a master's level clinician. However, the student with an undergraduate degree in psychology who earnestly pursues this particular career path will be rewarded by discovering a number of worthwhile positions offering the kind of client contact and caseload appropriate to his or her background and training. The following ad indicates a preference for someone with a master's degree, but will consider those candidates who do not have one. In the latter case, they probably will expect extensive experience.

Activities Therapist. (Medical center) function as member of multidisciplinary treatment team. Participate in diagnostic, assessment, & therapeutic process to deliver quality mental health services to psychiatric inpatients. Bachelor's degree (recreational therapy, art therapy, psychology), master's preferred.

Licensure and Certification

Some of these therapies warrant reimbursement by third-party payers under health insurance plans and others do not. Generally, in the case where third-party payment is involved, licensure, certification, and degree attainment of the therapist become critical issues in these treatment plans. The overwhelming majority of therapy is prescribed by a physician and the caregiver team. To ensure the continued professionalism of therapy, licensure, certification, and degree attainment are welcomed by most in the profession as ensuring their continued employment and demand by the public for their services.

Work Experience

Even in positions that accept an undergraduate degree in psychology, there may still be an expectation of fieldwork experience. For example, an addictions therapist position may be available for a candidate with a bachelor's degree in psychology, but that candidate should provide evidence of two years of outpatient counseling experience specific to drug and alcohol abuse and rehabilitation. Some of that experience may be achieved through well-supervised college internships and/or summer employment.

The work experience demanded can be quite specific and often there is a requirement that it be with the population described in the job advertisement. So, if the job is working with adults in a community residence and your experience has been with adolescents in a hospital setting, it may not be seen as appropriate preparation, given your degree level and lack of credentials.

Here is an advertisement for a cognitive therapist that is typical of its undergraduate degree requirement with an expectation of significant other experience with the client population (in this case, the disabled).

Cognitive Therapist. (Skilled nursing facility). We focus on psychosocial rehabilitation. Bachelor's degree in speech/language pathology, psychology, or related field. Experience working with the disabled and knowledge of computer-assisted therapeutic programs helpful.

Personal Qualifications

There are important personal qualities required by the majority of these therapist positions, and you'll need to be candid and realistic with yourself as you complete the self-assessment exercise that begins this book. Among the most important for skills therapists are:

- **Flexibility.** Some therapists work independently, while others are part of care teams. Because you are part of a team, there will be overlapping efforts, communication difficulties, and all the variables one encounters when the number of people involved in a project multiplies. You'll need to be open to changes on the spur of the moment with good grace and humor.

• **Patience.** All therapist positions require enormous reserves of patience. It is often painfully slow work, with small gains in the patient's progress that only the therapist and those working intimately with the client can appreciate.

• **Record keeping.** Record keeping is critical and meticulous. Process notes (records of your appointments with clients) may actually be subpoenaed in case of any litigation. There may be overall evaluations on your client by the entire team to which you will contribute. Charts, forms, insurance documentation, and other records of a client's treatment and progress need to be thoroughly maintained.

• **Listening.** We all can listen to some degree. Within the helping professions, where your client may or may not be able to communicate effectively or even authentically, you'll need well-developed listening skills to understand what the client is trying to tell you. To really listen to your clients, you need to care deeply about them and their needs.

• **Effective communication.** This is a frequently quoted skill on many résumés. Most college graduates feel they are effective communicators. You will be dealing with a variety of individuals, each communicating with you in a different way. Your communication not only needs to be clear and effective but "tuned in" to the person with whom you are working. You need to be sensitive to clients' understanding of you, the words they use, and what those words mean to them.

• **Empathy.** Listening and communicating with your clients involves understanding the world as they perceive it. Empathy means you share some degree of appreciation for what your client has experienced or feels. Truly understanding the other person's perceptions is a wonderful attribute for the helping professions.

• **Openness.** Understanding yourself and being able to express your own needs will help create trust and sharing. This does not mean you use the therapeutic situation to solve your problems, rather that you will be professional and open with your clients in your efforts to help them.

• **Acceptance.** In your work you may come across individuals whose behavior is reprehensible to you or whose values are very different from yours. To be a truly effective helper, you need to keep from imposing what you believe to be right or good on others and concentrate on how you can help this individual. You don't have to agree or accept the behavior, but you must believe in the dignity of the individual as worthy of help.

Earnings

A review of current job postings and conversations with hiring personnel show that salaries for entry-level therapy positions can vary widely, depending on the geographic location, type of facility, degree of experience, and level of autonomy required. Positions that involve some therapeutic modalities (under strict clinical supervision) range from a low of approximately $10 an hour to salaried positions between $22,000 and $30,000—with most positions falling within that range. Many of the positions are available at health-care facilities, and most of them pay a differential for evening, weekend, and holiday work hours. This salary range may seem shockingly low to some job seekers, but keep in mind these positions are usually carefully supervised by highly qualified professionals. In order to obtain a higher level of income, additional education, experience, and certification credentials will be required.

As we discussed in other career paths, it is especially important for you, the job seeker, to determine if the salary an organization is offering will be enough for you to support yourself. Your self-assessment can help you determine the level of pay you need to receive. And don't overlook the value of the benefits package, especially educational benefits, if you hope to grow in a therapy career path.

Career Outlook

The field of therapy as a career for the psychology graduate needs to be seen as one they may enter only "on approval." Demands will increase for more and more specialization and an increasingly higher level of credential for anyone involved in direct patient therapy. In the not too distant future, it probably will be impossible to enter this field without an advanced degree.

The essential and very understandable reason for such a push toward specialization, both in treatment and in credentials of the caregiver, is the overwhelming responsibility these individuals have, in part, for the health and well-being of their clients. The organizations (hospitals, benefit providers, rehabilitation centers, and doctors) who are ultimately responsible for the treatment plan of any one individual are subject to the risks involved in group work. Litigation against participants in all kinds of health issues abounds, and awards become increasingly astronomical and can have serious repercussions on the integrity and stature of those involved, regardless of their culpability.

One way of ensuring against this kind of risk is the very obvious one of demanding that the state set educational or professional criteria for the credentials of the participants. The future will only exacerbate this demand.

However, the psychology graduate who realizes this situation and who sees an immediate entry into the field as a preprofessional therapist as an exciting and demanding way to begin a career in psychology, can use this first job as a platform to grow and gain the necessary education and credentials to ensure continued professional-level employment

Strategy for Finding the Jobs

Your job search strategy for therapy positions must be based on a certain level of experience. This begins with completion of an internship. In addition, you should work to gain additional direct experience and read and study on your own to enhance your knowledge base. You also must be aware of certification and licensure issues and work toward acquiring those that are important for growth in your career.

Begin Gaining Experience Through an Internship

Your own college career center website will undoubtedly contain both internship listings and links to other promising internship sites at colleges and universities around the country. An additional resource may be one of the many internship directories published each year. A quick search on amazon.com, using the keyword "internship," brought up many directories. One to review is Peterson's *Internships* (revised yearly). The following is typical of the variety and scope of an internship:

Recreational Therapy Internship. (State Department of Mental Health). The recreational therapy internship meets the standards of the National Council for Therapeutic Recreation Certification (NCTRC) and the (state) Board of Recreation and Park Certification. The internship is 15 weeks in duration. We accept interns throughout the year with all start dates on the first Monday of the month. (State) hospital employs approximately thirty-five recreation therapists who work alongside art, dance, and music therapists in the Rehabilitation Therapy Service. Interns will work under a certified recreation therapist who is a member of an interdisciplinary treatment team. Interns will receive training and experience in: assessment completion, treatment planning, documentation of progress, and implementation of therapeutic recreation programming. Interns will also receive in-house training in the treatment of mental illness in a forensic setting. The intern will be required to present a research project to the Rehabilitation Therapy Professional Group at the end of the internship.

Students pursuing these kinds of experiences often do so because of their strong feelings that they would like to work directly with a client population in a more clinical, therapeutic manner to effect positive change. These experiences are usually fully supervised, and the student receives valuable feedback. An internship, such as the one cited above, or any similar hands-on experience will give you a solid understanding of the problems and challenges facing various client populations as well as the opportunity to build some specific helping skills.

Obtain Additional Related Work Experience
It appears that the key to working as a preprofessional in a field dominated by professionals is to approach the job search with some specifically related work experience. These need not all be paid positions. While still in college, you might consider volunteering at a mental health clinic or a drug halfway house. If your community has an Alcoholics Anonymous group that allows visitors (some do not), you might go and observe some meetings. Head Start, private and state rehabilitation clinics and hospitals, senior centers, and a host of other sites with differing populations and degrees of severity of problems may welcome your willingness to volunteer to help and may provide a broad range of experiences. Some may have part-time paid employment that you can fit into your schedule while in college.

In either case, use an experience such as this to its fullest advantage. Meet and talk with as many of the staff professionals as you can. Let them know of your interests and career aspirations. They'll have excellent advice and tips for you on employment, job searches, and job acquisitions.

Stay Aware of the Certification and Licensure Issues
Talk with colleagues and read up on the current dialogue in your field of therapy on certification and licensure. What is the direction in your state and how far are you from attaining the necessary stature to ensure your continued employment? If your employer offers educational benefits, you may want to consider working toward a master's degree at a nearby college or university.

To grow in your profession, both personally and in terms of your ability to act autonomously, to help design treatment programs, and to supervise other clinicians, you will eventually need to enhance your credentials with a master's degree. This will allow you to attain the kinds of licensure and/or certifications necessary to enjoy a broader range of employment possibilities and to enter private practice as well.

Read and Study on Your Own

Whatever milieu you find yourself in, don't be content with just your participation. Read and study what you can on the population and presenting problems. A site where you work on an internship or are employed part-time may house a professional library. Certainly the professional staff can provide you with insights on working with clients, and you can use your own academic training and library resources to discover as much as you can, in addition to the training and exposure you are receiving in your work position.

Possible Employers

If you are interested in working in a therapeutic capacity using your degree in psychology, be sure to explore the many types of organizations that may offer employment opportunities. Included here are medical institutions, schools, psychiatric facilities, private rehabilitation centers, residential care facilities, public and private mental health providers, nonprofit providers, and correctional facilities. Add to this list as you do your research, and be sure to network with administrators at the various types of sites where you would like to work.

Medical Institutions

One example of how the psychology major can put his or her interest in a therapeutic career in a medical institution to work is through occupational therapy. Many occupational therapy preprofessionals work in hospitals under the supervision of registered occupational therapists. They help people who have a disabling condition (mental, physical, developmental, or emotional) learn or regain skills necessary for daily living and working. In occupational therapy, a variety of techniques are used to help a client; for example, someone who experienced a brain injury in an auto accident can be helped to enhance his or her functioning.

Help in Locating These Employers. Nearly every type of therapy modality is employed in the many medical institutions that are found in this country. The American Hospital Association's website (aha.org) can help you locate any hospital or medical facility in the United States. Career books on any of the specific types of therapies, including *Opportunities in Occupational Therapy Careers* or the *Health Professions: Career and Education Directory*, will help you identify additional employment sites you may not have considered.

Schools

Therapeutic socialization programs for young children with Attention Deficit Hyperactivity Disorder (ADHD) utilize expressive and specifically art therapy in concert with a number of behavioral, cognitive, psychodynamic, and medical approaches. Arts activities can be used to explore various relational problems with peers, schoolmates, and families. Art, music, dance, and many other types of therapy can help students express things that may be difficult for them to put into words, or these therapies can help channel aggressive behaviors in a positive format.

Help in Locating These Employers. To help their students reach their full potential, there are many types of schools that hire various therapists and the preprofessionals who work with them. Be certain to review some of the excellent publications of the American Association for Employment in Education (aaee.org), including their *Job Search Handbook for Educators*. Ask the career professionals and librarians you are working with for the names of additional references.

Psychiatric Facilities

The American Art Therapy Association describes their profession as one that offers an opportunity to explore personal problems and potentials through verbal and nonverbal expression and to develop physical, emotional, and/or learning skills through therapeutic art experiences. Art therapy can be used in rehabilitation counseling to help psychiatric patients prepare for greater participation in the community. Patients may be easily frightened by the demands of today's society as they begin reintegration, and art therapy can help these patients express their feelings and work to overcome them.

Help in Locating These Employers. The Web is your best bet for the most current information on mental health services. At the time this book was published, looksmart.com was offering an online directory of mental health organizations and related associations listed nationally and by state. In addition, a prominent association is the National Association of State Mental Health Program Directors (nasmhpd.org). Click on Complete Membership Directory and enter a state name, and you'll see a list of possible contacts for that state. Then you could review the website of a given member's employer to find out about job openings.

Private Rehabilitation Centers

Massage therapy, or the art and science of applying the therapeutic properties of massage to restore function, relieve pain, prevent disability, and promote healing, is one therapy modality employed at private rehabilitation centers. A patient at this type of facility may receive massage therapy, along with several other types of therapy, on a daily basis as he or she recovers from one of a multitude of physical and/or mental conditions.

Help in Locating These Employers. An excellent introductory source that will, in turn, lead you to additional resources is the website soberrecovery .com, a resource for online alcohol addiction and mental health help. By entering the name of a state in the search box, you will see links to organizations, including private rehabilitation centers, that help people with compulsive gambling and substance abuse, just to name a few.

Residential Care Facilities

Residential care facilities often focus on a specific type of client they want to assist, and so the therapeutic modalities utilized will vary from location to location. Consider a residence that houses women who have left abusive relationships or a home for the mentally retarded who need low levels of support. Each utilizes appropriate therapies given the philosophy of the funding agency and the talents of the staff members.

Help in Locating These Employers. The American Network of Community Options and Resources (ancor.org) represents private providers who offer support and services to people with disabilities. Their website lists internships and career opportunities. You can also search their directory of members, and many have links to their websites that contain job postings. Begin with this site, but you may also want to examine specific state residential care sites such as the Association of Residential Resources in Minnesota (ARRM), which maintains a very professional site at arrm.org. One particularly attractive feature of the Minnesota site is its list of advocacy links. Check it out!

Public and Private Mental Health Providers

Horticultural therapy is an emerging type of rehabilitative therapy that involves using gardening techniques for either vocational rehabilitation or for leisure purposes. A progressive public or private mental health provider might employ therapists and qualified preprofessionals who utilize this modality to work with substance abusers who enjoy working outdoors or working with their hands. This helps clients find concrete and enjoyable outlets for negative feelings that need to be rechanneled.

Help in Locating These Employers. The state-by-state directory listings of not only mental health organizations but also mental health professional associations found at looksmart.com is an excellent one-stop resource to begin your search for public and private mental health providers. Click on Health and then Mental Health; you will see links to mental health practitioners, clinics, hospitals, and associations. Another comprehensive website is statelocalgov.net/index.cfm, which allows you to access the directories of every state in the United States. Locate the department of mental health to appreciate the services provided in that state and then access the human resources department for current job listings.

Nonprofit Providers

Nearly everyone, at some point in his or her life, will experience at least a temporarily (as opposed to a permanently) disabling condition and could benefit from working through one of the many types of therapies that are available. Quite a variety of nonprofit organizations provide funding or services that help people regain at least some level of functioning lost through a disabling condition or episode. Activities that employ drama therapy, or use psychodrama and dramatic productions to facilitate self-expression in clients, are funded by several nonprofit organizations.

Help in Locating These Employers. It would take you considerable time to thoroughly explore the nonprofit world. In a recent headline story of the journal *Advancing Philanthropy*, Canada was described as having the world's second-largest nonprofit sector, with the United States having the fifth largest. Two excellent websites to help you familiarize yourself with this important sector of the economy are guidestar.org and nonprofits.org. Then visit idea list.org to review current job listings.

Correctional Facilities

Dance, or movement therapy, is the psychotherapeutic use of movement to further the emotional, cognitive, and physical integration of the individual. Some preprofessional dance therapists work in correctional facilities helping inmates learn new ways to express themselves by using their bodies in movement, rather than aggressive tactics that are self-destructive.

Help in Locating These Employers. General career books that provide valuable information on working in corrections include *Careers in Social and Rehabilitation Services* and *Opportunities in Law Enforcement and Criminal Justice Careers*. Because correctional facilities are run by governmental units, other resources to examine include state websites. For federal jobs, go to bop.gov/jobs and search on such keywords as "recreation therapist," "recreation specialist," "education," and "vocational training specialist."

Possible Job Titles

Therapy job titles can range from generalist to specialist, depending on the modality that is used. Review the list provided here, and follow up on those that sound interesting by talking with a career counselor and a provider of that particular kind of therapy. You should also contact the professional association serving that type of therapist.

Activity therapist
Art specialist
Art therapist
Art therapy specialist
Behavior therapist
Clinician
Creative arts therapist
Creative therapist
Dance therapist
Day-treatment clinician
Drama therapist
Exercise therapist
Expressive therapist
Family therapist
Heat therapist
Horticultural therapist
Light therapist
Manual arts therapist
Marriage therapist
Movement therapist
Music therapist
Occupational therapist

Psychiatric rehabilitation counselor
Psychomotor therapist
Recreational therapist
Recreation specialist
Therapist
Voice therapist
Water therapist

Related Occupations

As you consider the many skills required of therapists, including flexibility, patience, record keeping, listening, effective communication, empathy, openness, and acceptance, you will realize that these same skills are valued in other types of workers. You'll be able to immediately name some, but review the samples shown below to see if you've considered each of these job titles.

Community and social service worker
Credit counselor
Human services worker
Mediator
Negotiator
Project director
Residential care worker
Safety coordinator
Special services supervisor
Teacher

If you review your self-assessment, you can probably add to this list based on the deeper understanding you've built of yourself.

Professional Associations

Some of the specific associations that oversee certification and licensing for some of the therapy modalities we've discussed are shown on the following pages. Each provides information on gaining specific training and education beyond the bachelor's degree and will provide career information to those who request it.

American Art Therapy Association
1202 Allanson Rd.
Mundelein, IL 60060
arttherapy.org
Members/Purpose: Art therapists, students, and individuals in related fields
dedicated to the belief that the creative process involved in art making is
healing and life enhancing
Training: Annual conference, regional symposia, continuing education
opportunities
Journals/Publications: *Art Therapy: Journal of the American Art Therapy
Association*; *AATA Newsletter*; membership directory
Job Listings: Members can access job opportunity listings online

**American Association for Marriage and
  Family Therapy**
112 S. Alfred St.
Alexandria, VA 22314
aamft.org
Members/Purpose: Professional society of marriage and family therapists;
provides individuals with the tools and resources they need to succeed as
marriage and family therapists
Training: Hosts an annual national training conference each fall and a
weeklong series of continuing education institutes in the summer
Journals/Publications: *Journal of Marital and Family Therapy*; news about
the field in *Family Therapy Magazine*
Job Listings: Offers AAMFT Job Connection to members

American Dance Therapy Association
2000 Century Plaza, Suite 108
10632 Little Patuxent Pkwy.
Columbia, MD 21044
adta.org
Members/Purpose: Individuals professionally practicing dance therapy,
students interested in becoming dance therapists, university departments
with dance therapy programs, and individuals in related therapeutic
fields; stimulates communication among dance/movement therapists and
members of allied professions
Training: Conducts workshops
Journals/Publications: *American Journal of Dance Therapy*; *ADTA*
newsletter; online directory of members

American Horticultural Therapy Association
3570 E. 12th Ave., Suite 206
Denver, CO 80206
ahta.org
Members/Purpose: Professional horticultural therapists and rehabilitation specialists; horticultural therapy students; institutions and commercial organizations
Training: Lists meetings and training opportunities on website
Journals/Publications: *Journal of Therapeutic Horticulture*
Job Listings: Members can view current job postings

American Massage Therapy Association
500 Davis St.
Evanston, IL 60201
amtamassage.org
Members/Purpose: Massage therapists, technicians, and students; works to establish massage therapy as integral to the maintenance of good health and complementary to other therapeutic processes
Training: Lists schools and continuing education opportunities on website
Journals/Publications: *Massage Therapy Journal*
Job Listings: Available on website

American Music Therapy Association
8455 Colesville Rd., Suite 1000
Silver Spring, MD 20910
musictherapy.org
Members/Purpose: Certified music therapists; students in music therapy, colleges and universities offering music therapy programs; and individuals interested in the field; certifies music therapists
Journals/Publications: *Journal of Music Therapy*; *Music Therapy Perspectives*; *AMTA Member Sourcebook*
Job Listings: Job opportunities list available online to members

American Occupational Therapy Association
4720 Montgomery Lane
P.O. Box 31220
Bethesda, MD 20824
aota.org
Members/Purpose: Occupational therapists, occupational therapy assistants, and students who provide services to people whose lives have

been disrupted by physical injury or illness, developmental problems, the aging process, or social or psychological difficulties

Journals/Publications: *American Journal of Occupational Therapy*; AJOT Online; *OT Practice Magazine*

Job Listings: Website contains job listings

American Physical Therapy Association
1111 N. Fairfax St.
Alexandria, VA 22314
apta.org

Members/Purpose: Professional organization of physical therapists and physical therapist assistants and students; fosters the development and improvement of physical therapy service, education, and research

Journals/Publications: *Physical Therapy*; *PT—Magazine of Physical Therapy*

Job Listings: Online job listings

National Association for Drama Therapy
15 Post Side Lane
Pittsford, NY 14534
nadt.org

Members/Purpose: Drama therapists and others interested in the field of drama therapy, including those in psychotherapy, rehabilitation, and education professions; develops criteria and standards of training for drama therapists; maintains a system of registration and peer review

Training: Sponsors national conference and other educational events

Journals/Publications: *Dramascope*

Job Listings: Job postings under News on website

National Therapeutic Recreation Society
22377 Belmont Ridge Rd.
Ashburn, VA 20148
nrpa.org/content/default.aspx?documentId=530

Members/Purpose: A branch of the National Recreation and Park Association; includes practitioners, administrators, educators, volunteers, students, and consumers; specializes in the provision of therapeutic recreation services for persons with disabilities in clinical facilities and in the community

Training: Offers a variety of institutes and schools

Journals/Publications: *Therapeutic Recreation Journal*

Job Listings: Link to Career Center job listings to website

10

Path 5: Teaching

Perhaps the most familiar career path for those considering using their psychology education as a primary skill would be college teaching. It is certainly the role model for employment that psychology students have seen most often, and it may be that a particular teacher was the inspiration for their choice of a major in college.

It is an attractive life to work with a body of information you love, and to share that enjoyment with countless students through the years. There is learning for the instructor, as well, which adds its own excitement. Most teachers readily admit that they enjoy being students, and good teachers come to the classroom as ready to learn from students as students arrive hoping to learn from their teachers. Good teachers maintain a regular program of professional development, continuing to learn new classroom techniques, improve their teaching methods, and add to their body of knowledge.

In any academic institution, there is a fellowship and camaraderie among teachers. They share anecdotes about techniques that have or have not worked in the classroom, and many can also share an interest in the growth and development of particular students they have interacted with through the years. Students often come back and visit their formative teachers, which brings its own rewards to the teacher.

Talk to psych professors you know and they'll tell you a surprising fact about their profession. They don't teach psychology, they teach students! The art of teaching and the skills required in handling the dynamics of student interaction are equally as important as knowledge of the course content. Your psychology classroom will be populated with many students majoring in psychology and your presentation of this material will weigh heavily in their consideration of continuing their studies in the major. But you'll also have many nonmajors who are taking your course as a general education requirement or for a minor, who represent different ages, cultural backgrounds, biases, and issues, and who sit in your class with dramatically different degrees of interest in the subject and the teacher. With all that in the way, simply having a love of psychology yourself is not enough, though that is certainly important and desirable. How could you begin to teach something you didn't truly enjoy and expect not to convey that disinterest through a mechanical approach to the subject?

Teaching something is an entirely different art beyond knowing something, and it demands additional skills. It has very little to do with your own proficiency in the subject. The world is full of extremely skillful practitioners who, for one reason or another—and quite often inexplicably—cannot teach someone how they do it. The practice of something is very different from professing it in a classroom.

For example, planning for learning outcomes is critical. Teaching psychology within an established college curriculum means corresponding to some departmental goals and course outlines. Unless you've designed the course, there will be a written course description in the catalog. To accomplish this body of learning within a set time period requires judicious planning of the material. What will be done each day? How much time should be allowed between assignments, readings, and labs? Which materials should be required and which only recommended? Scores of decisions must be made about how material will be introduced, presented, and ultimately delivered back to you for evaluation.

Add in that students learn in different ways. Some are auditory learners who enjoy listening and gain most of their information in this way. If they are required to take notes and listen, something may have to give, and it may be difficult for them to retain the material. Others prefer a visual approach with board work, videos, handouts, their own notes, diagrams, books, and many other visual materials. They retain these images and can call them up to remember the material.

Still other students learn best by participating through reading in class, role plays, team projects, and other activities that physically involve them. These are kinesthetic learners, and they are often forgotten in planning and curriculum design. The professional teacher ensures that the class satisfies the learning styles of all the students through judicious combinations of teaching modalities. The professional teacher has analyzed his or her own teaching style and seeks to incorporate those other elements that come less naturally to ensure all students are reached.

The teaching and learning that take place in a class are not static. For the student and the instructor, the classroom is an emotionally charged environment that may call into play questions of self-esteem and competency. People are exploring new definitions of themselves in relation to their capabilities, values, or achievements. A good teacher understands this and encourages a risk-free environment of mutual appreciation and participation. Both teacher and student are allowed to make mistakes and move on. The teacher strives to assist in establishing congruence between the self (who we know we are right now), the ideal self (who we want to be), and the learning environment being created in the classroom. Hopefully, the classroom will be a place where the student can rise up and begin to attain his or her ideal self.

Any mention of competency, self-esteem, or self-worth naturally suggests the subject of grading and the evaluation teachers provide. Grades are an expected and required part of many institutional academic settings. Establishing fair and consistent standards of evaluating your students and assigning grades is a significant challenge to many teachers who otherwise feel perfectly competent in the teaching role. Students, too, often complain about grading practices in teachers whom they, in every other respect, have positive feelings about.

The teacher of psychology is called upon to play other roles, too. Animating the class and inspiring attention and commitment to the material are all required in teaching. Part of this is the teacher's enthusiasm, part is teaching style, and part is effective use of ancillary materials and the ability to relate this material to a student's life. Psychology teachers, of course, present information and demonstrate the psychological perspectives, the psychology of developmental stages, and a variety of approaches to the diagnosis, treatment, and care of those people who have a mental illness or a handicap. They seek to raise relevant questions, prompt dialogues within the class, and develop within students the discipline of self-questioning. They clarify difficulties or obscurities in the material and draw parallels or find relationships between examples.

For a professional teacher, each class is not only an opportunity to teach the subject, but also to teach how to learn as well. How to question, how to record information, how to be selective, and how to retain information is an ongoing lesson that takes place in every classroom to some degree.

Good teachers also use the class and the material to explain how this material reflects feelings. They will share their own agreement with or support of ideas or emotions in the material under study. Most of all, instructors will evaluate and, by example, develop the student's capacity for self-evaluation through careful, caring feedback about both in-class and out-of-class work. The instructor's own examples of preparation, organization, personal appearance, evaluation standards, student interest, and enthusiasm will remain examples long after the memory of the actual class content may have faded.

Teachers are very frequently cited as important factors in our choice of a career. Very often teachers will remember one or two of their teachers who were strong influences on their decision to teach. Much of that influence was a result of their presence in the classroom. They served as models of people enjoying what they were doing and doing it skillfully. They were professional and correct, yet remained natural and approachable. We could watch and listen to them and think, "Maybe I could do that."

Definition of the Career Path

We'll focus on two levels of degree attainment in this teaching career path: the master's degree and the doctoral degree. Both degree earners will find employment in college settings; however, the doctorate in psychology is preeminently the degree of choice and will make the largest number of positions available to you. Even here, however, there are caveats because the specialization possibilities at both the master's and doctoral levels in psychology are dizzying, and many faculty position descriptions that we will present in this section are specific in the research interests they hope an applicant will add to their faculty.

Areas of Specialization
Teachers of psychology can focus their research and teaching efforts in at least one of many different areas, including:

Adolescent psychology
Applied psychology
Child/family behavior therapy
Clinical psychology
Cognitive and human memory
Community mental health
Counseling psychology
Cross-cultural psychology
Developmental psychobiology

Developmental psychology
Differential diagnosis
Environmental psychology
Experimental social psychology
Forensic assessment
History of psychology
Humanistic psychology
Hypnotherapy
Industrial psychology
Medical psychology
Neuropsychology
Perception
Physiological psychology
Psychiatric rehabilitation
Psychology of aging
Psychology of imagery
Psychology of self
Psychotherapy
Social psychology
Systems of psychology

Some of these areas may be vaguely familiar to you from your under-graduate survey courses. Others are completely foreign. It can be a bewil-deringly long list, and even if some of these specialties do seem interesting, you are probably asking yourself, "How do you become knowledgeable about these areas?" The answer in most cases is in the early days of your graduate degree work. You may be in a doctoral program that does not necessarily require a stopping-off point at the master's level, or you may decide to begin with a master's degree and then reevaluate your position before launching yourself on the doctoral course. For many, there is a change of university affiliation between the master's and doctoral degrees that comes about in search of a particular field of study or to associate with a department known for some research focus or simply to expose oneself to new faculty with new perspectives.

Teaching with a Master's Degree

Interestingly enough, there are college positions for those with a master's degree in psychology. Review this job description, which presents specific demands for expertise within psychology as well:

> **Instructor, Psychology.** Teaches assigned courses in accordance with course competencies & syllabi. Utilizes variety of instructional strategies, techniques, & delivery methods. Fosters safe & civil learning environment. Develops & maintains current course syllabi & outlines. Participates in college & program projects, events, & committee work. Monitors, evaluates, & documents student attendance, progress, & competency attainment; submits related reports as required. Maintains established office hours. Participates in ongoing development & revision of curriculum & course materials & competencies, & in selection of textbooks & other instructional materials. Requires master's degree in psychology.

Similar positions, even those requiring a high level of specialization, can be found in community colleges or schools with smaller enrollments. A rewarding teaching career in psychology at the college level with a master's degree is possible. Two-year and community college work can provide a long and productive career within the same institution or provide the opportunity for a lateral move to a similar type of institution. At the same time, however, it is important to caution you that if you are interested in moving from that type of institution to a four-year college or university, it may be difficult without an advanced degree, despite the fact that you may have years of teaching experience.

There also are some teaching jobs at the four-year college level with a master's degree in psychology. Nevertheless, the movement, expectation, and market demand would be for the doctoral degree, and it is that degree that will provide the most security in terms of employment and employment opportunities at the college and university level.

Teaching with a Doctoral Degree

The doctoral degree in psychology opens up the world of college and university teaching to the prospective educator. Competition here is keen for positions advertised in publications such as *The Chronicle of Higher Education* (chronicle.com), a weekly newspaper reporting on higher-education issues and containing the most complete listing of faculty, staff, and leadership position openings for colleges and universities in the United States and some foreign countries. The following are ads from *The Chronicle* that would be of interest to a new Ph.D. in psychology.

The road to a doctorate is fairly long and arduous. It is hard work. Along the way, you'll meet some wonderful people, some who'll be friends and colleagues the rest of your life. Even colleagues separated by long distances have

Psychologist. Tenure-track position. Teach in one or more of the following areas: Social Psychology, Psychometrics, Learning and Cognition, Developmental, and other courses of interest. Obtain research/training grants and involve students in research projects. Ph.D. required.

Psychology Professor. Entry-level, one-year appointment with possibility of longer-term employment. Earned doctorate required. We seek scholar with broad interests who can teach variety of undergraduate courses including abnormal psychology, history and systems of psychology, and human cognition and memory.

Faculty Position in Psychology. Tenure track position in Cognitive Psychology. Seek applicants who have potential to develop productive research program in general area of cognition, with preference for candidates with research interests in higher-order cognition and individual differences. We welcome candidates with interest or expertise in functional magnetic resonance imaging. Applicants who share broad orientation to theory, research, and application are encouraged to apply.

the opportunity to revisit at conferences and symposia. Creating and maintaining this network plays an important role in the work of academicians.

The Earned Doctorate Versus ABD

All of these ads are interesting because they require an earned doctorate. To apply, you must have your degree in hand. Some advertisements will encourage the application of ABD (All But Dissertation) candidates who have not yet, but are soon, to complete their degree work. A position requiring an earned doctorate will pay more than an ABD position and will lead more directly and quickly to possible tenure and promotion. The ABD candidate will also have to decide how they will finish their degree (the dissertation often being the most time-consuming aspect of their academics) and hold down a full-time job.

Especially in psychology, because of the sensitive nature of the material being presented, colleges and universities of even modest size are going to seek the most credentialed and skilled faculty they can find and afford. Larger and more prestigious schools with significant research agendas will be even more demanding of the background of their faculty.

You'll have opportunities to write, teach, and perhaps publish—all before you finish your degree. Take advantage of these opportunities when you can.

As the advertisements suggest, some of those kinds of qualifications will be asked of you. However, be selective, as it is possible to become overly involved in some of these areas to the detriment of your degree progress.

Other Issues for Teachers of Psychology

Many of the ads we provide suggest issues important for those with master's and doctoral degrees.

- Demonstrating cultural sensitivity
- Documenting teaching effectiveness
- Developing a track record in research, publications, and presentations
- Providing community service

Position descriptions such as those provided throughout this path allow candidates to approach the hiring process with their eyes wide open.

Demonstrating Cultural Sensitivity

Some of the advertisements make demands for cultural sensitivity. This is prompted in part by the location of the school advertising for faculty. They may have a student body that is highly diverse. In other cases, it is a sincere attempt on the hiring institution's part to increase sensitivity and awareness of the diversity that exists beyond the campus. Here's an advertisement for a psychology professorship from *The Chronicle of Higher Education* that speaks specifically to the diversity possible in the classroom:

Entry-Level Social or Community Psychologist. Located downtown, _____ College is a diverse, open-access undergraduate and graduate urban institution. Seeking completed Ph.D. for tenure-track position. Responsibilities include full-time teaching load, scholarship and professional activity, and service to the college and community. Teaching experience at undergraduate level required.

If you were teaching in a multicultural class with an Asian complement to the student body, it would be highly inappropriate and a good example of cultural bias to indicate in a class discussion on symptomatic behavior that a failure to make direct and sustained eye contact with a physician was significant. Many Asian races do not make direct eye contact except to intimates and even more seldom to authority figures.

Gender-biased language, ignorance of cultures and customs, and inconsiderate choice of texts or illustrative materials from a diversity perspective only serve to impugn your teaching and undermine your credibility. It is in your best interest to broaden your horizons and ensure your class is an inclusive and welcoming one.

Documenting Teaching Effectiveness

In one ad, documentation of positive student evaluations is requested. This could come from graduate teaching assistantships done while working on the doctoral degree. Many students acquire this experience as part-time faculty, lecturers, or adjunct faculty. Summaries of student-teaching evaluations that you received while gaining this experience can be used to document teaching success.

Developing a Track Record in Research, Publications, and Presentations

Some institutions of higher learning emphasize the teaching role and do not put excessive demands on faculty to "publish or perish." Other institutions place a high value on research and publications and a determined effort by faculty exists to find good research projects and then publish their findings.

It is important to mention here that, regardless of the posture of your institution regarding research and publications, as a teacher you should have an interest in sharing what you know with a larger audience. This may be accomplished through writing books, articles, or monographs. It also can be achieved through public presentations at seminars, workshops, and conferences, depending on what suits your style best. In questions of promotion and tenure, your record of sharing your technical and professional expertise will be examined.

Providing Community Service

Colleges and universities have always been part of the larger communities in which they reside. Faculty and staff are often called upon to give back to the community that houses them. This can take many forms for the institution: an annual clean-up day or allowing local organizations to use performing spaces or open fields for special events.

For the psychology faculty, the need for outreach is very great. Local counseling hotlines may need staffers or someone to train the staffers. Any number of local shelters or halfway houses may need skilled volunteers to take client histories or do referrals with other helping agencies. Teen drop-in sexuality information clinics, local civic groups needing speakers, a variety of board of trustee opportunities—all of these could benefit from the psychology faculty member's involvement and attention.

How Long Does It Take to Get a Doctorate?

There has been considerable discussion in academic circles about the length of time to degree for individuals enrolled in doctoral programs. In an article found on the American Psychological Association's website, it was reported that psychology Ph.D.s spent a median 7.3 years getting their doctorate. Across all disciplines, the median was 7.5 years. The article notes, however, that time to completion varies by psychology subfield. Review the federal report, "Doctorate Recipients from United States Universities," which offers data on most Ph.D. recipients (http://caspar.nsf.gov). Not all students who begin a Ph.D. program complete it, so there is a corresponding rate of mortality that goes along with this issue of time-to-degree.

The important point is that doctoral work comes at a time in many young people's lives when, after sixteen or more years of education, no matter how fascinating the advanced study, distractions occur. These distractions may be relationships, a strong biological imperative to begin a family, economic pressures to leave school and earn an income, or simply fatigue. Consequently, the dropout rate has been disappointingly high, especially when doctoral programs are not sufficiently explicit about requirements and the time it takes to complete a degree.

Working Conditions

The working conditions for college psychology teachers vary according to the institution, but there is enough commonality that we can make some generalizations. Many people consider a college teaching environment one of the most attractive work settings imaginable. There is less need to appease a number of outside publics—no school board to satisfy, no parents, no parent-teacher groups. Students are there voluntarily, and the upper-level classes are populated with psychology majors who love their subject and are interested in doing the work required to succeed in their courses.

Academic Freedom

The world of the college classroom is closed to outsiders. It is, in fact, rare to have a class interrupted by anyone outside of the room, so understood is this convention. Generally, the concept of academic freedom has allowed professors to express themselves within their class material with far greater pointedness than is the case in other teaching environments, and the system protects their right to do so. However, an increasing number of successful lawsuits and harassment claims are being made by students against faculty for what they perceive to be an improper use of the teaching platform. On campuses where this has occurred, concern and debate continue.

Grading, evaluation procedures, number of tests, and even the issue of whether to have textbooks is entirely up to the faculty member, and if the rationale supports his or her decisions, the university often will not interfere.

All of these conditions make the classroom environment and the relations of faculty and students very different than what has come before in the student's education.

Tenure

An added protection is the granting of tenure to established professors who have documented significant teaching histories and excellent student reviews, publications, campus committee work, and outreach to the community. The granting of tenure adds an additional degree of job security and further supports their expression of academic freedom. Colleges and universities have strict guidelines for promotion and tenure that may put strong emphasis and pressure on the faculty member to write, do research, deliver papers at professional meetings, and become involved in outreach to the community and with in-college service.

Administrative Duties

In some departments the role of chair of the department is rotated, and all faculty are expected to serve a term. In other institutions, the chair is a hotly contested office.

Department-chair duties involve overseeing the scheduling of each semester's courses and assigning faculty responsibility for those course offerings. These duties may include hiring part-time faculty and adjuncts to meet demand or replace faculty on sabbatical or negotiating with other administrators for additional classroom space.

Supervision of the department budget is the chair's responsibility, and this includes monitoring expenditures for supplies, special events, faculty development, and travel. Faculty often lobby intensely for travel and professional development funds from the chair, who must exercise impartiality and discretion in administering these funds.

Department meetings are called and run by the chair, who sets the meeting's agenda. These meetings may be as frequent as every week and even in large departments will occur monthly.

Many colleges and universities hold a council of chairs to address issues such as curriculum changes, general education requirements, faculty standards, and other interrelated issues.

Facilities and Support

Facilities tend to be excellent, including laboratories, and there is usually adequate support staff to type materials, do copying, and prepare testing materials. A private office is usually provided, and a varied menu of faculty privileges may be available. Computers are usually provided for writing, research, library access, and data manipulation.

Work Schedule

The actual teaching time in a college or university setting involves about ten class hours per week. At an institution that focuses on faculty research, the teacher would be responsible for teaching two to three courses that each meet three to four hours per week. Schools that emphasize teaching rather than research require instructors to teach three to four courses for a total of nine to twelve hours of class time per week. These class hours and some mandated office hours for advising class students and general advisees are the principal requirements for attendance on the faculty member's part. But as the ads below make clear, there are other expectations.

Psychology. Teaching responsibilities in the areas of research methods, advanced experimental, sensation and perception, and other undergraduate courses in an area of interest that matches departmental goals. Commitment to undergraduate research preparation of psychology majors is of primary importance. Interest in integrating multicultural and diversity issues into psychology courses and fostering a climate open to students from diverse backgrounds. Undergraduate advising. Additional responsibilities may include faculty adviser for Psychology Club/Psi Chi and coordinator of preprofessional focus. Doctorate completed by June 1 required. Prefer Ph.D. in psychology.

Psychology. Tenure-track position. Child-clinical psychology with an ability to teach courses in developmental psychopathology, child therapy, general psychology, and other teaching, as well as research and service to the academic community.

A college day is certainly not a rigid routine. Class schedules are fixed, but beyond those much is up to the involvement and activity level of each faculty member. Certainly, days can be busy and long. The college teacher may feel institutional and professional pressures to fulfill certain roles, but the actual election of how to do that is up to the individual. Classes, office hours, meetings, and research work will be required. Because college campuses are often wonderful centers of art, music, and intellectual exchange, there are frequently events to attend in the evening. Faculty members may act as advisers to fraternities, sororities, campus newspapers, or clubs, which also adds to their day.

Teaching Introductory Courses

Most advertisements also indicate that the successful candidate will be teaching general psychology classes. Teaching Introduction to Psychology classes is generally part of the teaching load of new college psychology faculty. Many of the students will be taking Introduction to Psychology because it is a college requirement for graduation and part of a general education core curriculum and not because they are psychology majors or have deliberately chosen the course. The psychology department performs a service to the entire college in offering this course. For many students, regardless of how they found their way to the class, this introductory course may prove to be an exciting introduction to a field of study they had not considered previously. Many majors are introduced through these generally required courses. Even senior faculty will teach at least one offering of introduction to psychology, though as you become more senior in the faculty you can take on courses that are more directly related to your interests and educational background.

Scholarly Research

In addition to courses and advising, scholarly research is expected even at colleges that do not base tenure on publication. All colleges want their faculty to contribute to the scholarly dialogue in their discipline, and this involvement is reviewed by chairs of departments and academic deans periodically throughout the instructor's career. It may be a determining element in granting tenure or promotion to that faculty member and may influence issues such as salary negotiations and merit increases.

Committee Work

Committee work is also important because the faculty at most colleges are the governing and rule-making bodies who determine governance and program changes. Committee work can be issue oriented, such as a commission on the status of women or a female faculty pay-equity survey; it may be programmatic, such as a committee to study the core curriculum for undergraduates or to devise a new graphic arts major; it might be related to credentials, as in a committee set up to prepare materials for an accreditation visit.

Some committees, such as those involving academic standards, curriculum review, promotion and tenure, and planning and administrator-review, are permanent, though the members may change on a rotating schedule. Other groups are formed for a limited time or until completion of some task. These committees are essential and are one vehicle for guiding the direction of the school. Having the support of all the faculty and constantly fresh and interested members helps to ensure all voices are heard and many different opinions are considered in making what are often far-reaching decisions.

Training and Qualifications

Most four-year colleges and universities require that job candidates possess a doctorate in psychology and usually will, in addition, look for specialized areas of research, publication, prior teaching, and/or clinical experience. Occasionally, a college will hire faculty on a nontenured basis with less than a doctoral degree, but generally, the larger the institution, the less likely this will happen. Salary and assignments may be affected by lack of an earned doctorate.

If a faculty member is hired without an earned doctoral degree, there may be a stipulation in the hiring contract indicating how much time can elapse before the degree must be earned. The difficulty here would then be your ability to finish the degree (for many the dissertation is the most challenging and time-consuming aspect of the degree) while holding down a full-time job. This certainly needs to be considered in your negotiations.

Seasoned scholars work with students at the very senior levels of graduate work for both master's and doctoral degrees. These scholars enhance their own unique areas of expertise as students pursue their degrees. Classes may be very small at this level, even at a large university, and the work is highly collaborative. Your teaching work at this level may be reduced to allow for pure research and writing in your areas of interest and scholarship, and you will be called upon frequently to speak to professional and scholarly groups about that research.

Earnings

Major salary surveys, such as those for faculty positions, usually lag by at least two years. At the time this book was published, the average assistant professor salary for psychology positions at four-year colleges was $38,733 and at universities, $46,408. Instructors who are ABD earn a mean salary of $32,250. Salary will vary by discipline taught and by geographic location of a given position. The American Psychological Association's website (apa.org) offers salary survey information as well as a wealth of other information for students interested in pursuing a graduate degree and using it to teach.

Career Outlook

As you consider employment in academe, one important trend worth researching is the increasing use of part-time faculty. In 1970, 22 percent of the professoriat worked part-time. As we begin the twenty-first century, part-time and temporary faculty now constitute a majority of all those teaching in colleges and universities. There are many reasons for the shift, but the bottom line for you is that there is heavy competition for full-time positions in higher education.

Other factors worth researching are current trends in the use of tenure; population trends and the resulting number of students expected to attend college; whether a minimum faculty retirement age is currently required; and the number of individuals currently pursuing advanced degrees in psychology.

Given your investment of time and financial resources you have much to consider. Both *The Chronicle of Higher Education*'s website (chronicle.org) and the American Association of University Professors' website (aaup.org) will have the latest information on these topics.

Strategy for Finding the Jobs

After you have invested so many years in acquiring the educational credentials required for teaching psychology in higher education, you will want to
be sure to employ a useful strategy for gaining work. This strategy should
include being prepared to relocate, getting your curriculum vitae in shape,
using well-established job listings such as *The Chronicle of Higher Education*,
networking with faculty colleagues, and attending professional meetings.
Be sure to enhance your strategy as you decide on the area of psychology
you will specialize in by talking with mentors and career development
professionals.

Be Prepared to Relocate

Acquiring a college teaching position in psychology nearly always means that
you will have to relocate to an institution other than where you received your
degree. Higher education has limited openings at any one time. You increase
your opportunities for securing a college teaching post as you expand the
boundaries of where you will consider relocating.

Like many graduate students, you may have enjoyed teaching part-time
at your degree-granting institution. Often, there is an opportunity to teach
as an adjunct faculty member for a limited period. Adjunct positions are used
to staff introductory courses or to complete staffing shortages during national
searches for permanent full-time faculty. Adjunct or part-time work is wonderful experience and will be an excellent recommendation to an institution
considering your application. It is seldom, however, a guarantee of earning
a full-time spot at your own school.

Most psychology departments have budget "lines" dedicated to full-time
tenured faculty. This means that faculty who are hired in those budget lines
are hired with the expectation they will become permanent members of the
faculty and earn tenure and promotion when they are qualified. Consequently,
although there may be schools you would enjoy teaching at or areas of the
country where you would prefer to live, the supply and demand of college
professorships clearly dictates you must follow the demand and relocate.

Though it may be disappointing to feel your job search is completely dic-
tated by marketplace demands, if you talk to some of your own faculty mentors, you will learn how it was for them in their job search. Most of them
have relocated as well. In our conversations with faculty colleagues, time and
again they will mention their real pleasure at discovering a new area of the
country, new activities, and new awarenesses as they moved with their careers.
College communities the world over tend to be centers of exchange, with

speakers, arts events, celebrations, and a year-round calendar of activities for people of all ages and interests. Because of the college population, many have good shopping and excellent services. They are wonderful communities in which to live, raise a family, and retire.

Get Your Curriculum Vitae in Shape

Higher education places some different demands on the job seeker. In place of the résumé, teaching candidates use a document called the curriculum vitae. It's a Latin term that means "the course of one's life." A curriculum vitae shares many similarities with the résumé but also some significant differences.

Many job seekers in higher education forget some of the résumé, or in this case, curriculum vitae basics as they begin their job search. Candidates tend to focus on their educational, teaching, research, and other experiences, often overlooking some of the very basic techniques that are critical for this document.

The academic job search is competitive, and no matter how excellent your credentials, you still need to assemble a package of materials that is professional, accurate, and complete, and will make an impact on the selection committee reviewing it. Ask yourself the following questions:

1. Have you customized your vitae for each position you apply for? If not, you should. Each advertisement reflects what type of background is important for that position, and your vitae should clearly announce, "I have the background and experiences you are seeking!" So, if multicultural awareness is mentioned as a need and you have served on a diversity task force, be certain that you list it on your vitae.

2. Is your document neat and easily read? Too much text with little white space or margins invites fatigue. You may have to go to additional pages to create an inviting format.

3. Does your document look inviting or forbidding? Bright white paper with black lettering is hard on the eyes. Choose a soft cream or off-white to soften the contrast.

4. Will the selection committee be able to identify the categories of information you have included on your résumé? Use bold letters, underlining, and indented sections to help accomplish this. Your campus career office can provide good guidance on these technical aspects of your curriculum vitae.

5. Have you organized and listed relevant course work according to what the institution is asking you to teach? Remember, readers of English read

from top to bottom, and in scanning a vitae, committee members may only read the first couple items on a list, or the first phrase of a description. Always place the most salient information first.

Exhibit 10.1 is a sample curriculum vitae that might be typical for a newly minted Ph.D. in psychology seeking a first permanent teaching position in higher education. Your college career office will have many additional samples, and you can also review the book *How to Prepare Your Curriculum Vitae*.

Exhibit 10.1
SAMPLE CURRICULUM VITAE

WENDY PALMS
Curriculum Vitae

18 Main St.
San Francisco, CA 04131
(415) 555-5555

EDUCATION	Ph.D., Human Development & Family Studies, 2006 Cornell University, Ithaca, NY Bachelor of Arts Degree in Psychology, 1999 Pomona College, Claremont, CA
SCHOLARSHIPS & HONORS	NICHD Traineeship in Cognitive Development Cornell University, 1998–1999 Mortar Board, Pomona College, 1998
TEACHING	Lecturer, University of Manitoba, 2004–2006 General Psychology, Child Development, Adolescent Development Teaching Assistant, Cornell University, 2003–2004 General Psychology
PROFESSIONAL ORGANIZATIONS	American Psychological Association —Division: Developmental Psychology —Division: Teaching of Psychology Society for Research in Child Development

PUBLICATIONS	Palms, W. J. "Formal operational reasoning and the primary effect in impression formation," *Developmental Psychology*, 2005.
	Will, J. P., and W. J. Palms. "Social cognition and social relationships in early adolescence." *International Journal of Behavioral Development*, 1996.
SUBMITTED FOR PUBLICATION	Palms, W. J. "Who goes with whom? Early adolescent girls' perceptions of peer group structure."
PAPERS	Palms, W. J. "Formal operational reasoning and the primacy effect in impression formation." Doctoral dissertation, Cornell University, 2006.
	Palms, W. J. "Formal operational reasoning and the primacy effect in impression formation." Paper presented at the biennial meeting of the Society for Research in Child Development, 2004.
	Palms, W. J. "Variables related to patterns of social exchange." Paper presented at the annual meeting of the American Psychological Association, 2004.
COMMITTEES	Graduate School Council Cornell University, 2002–2004
	Student Representative, Board of Trustees Pomona College, 1998–1999
REFERENCES	Furnished upon request.

Go to "The Source" to Review Job Listings

The Chronicle of Higher Education is the weekly national publication listing junior college, four-year college, and university teaching positions in psychology. Your career center, department office, and college library will have copies you can review weekly. *The Chronicle* is also available online (chronicle.com). In addition, use your favorite search engine and enter key words such as faculty jobs, and you will be directed to a number of position listings.

Network with Faculty Colleagues

Another excellent resource for college-level positions are the faculty colleague contacts you make as you pursue your advanced degree. There is a well-established network that becomes very active when schools are seeking to fill a position. Many search committees rely on the personal recommendation of a friend or former teaching associate to do the very best by the hiring institution.

This is a referral network, not a placement service. Your colleagues will be suggesting your name as an applicant. There are no guarantees, and all positions at this level must go through a search committee and interviews. Nevertheless, a recommendation to apply from a colleague is a strong beginning. For this reason, it's important to ensure that your faculty mentors and colleagues are well aware of your teaching and research interests and geographic preferences so they can respond for you and move the process along if an opportunity presents itself.

Attend Professional Meetings

Professional meetings, seminars, and conferences allow you to meet and listen to representatives from many institutions. You become aware of research initiatives and many of the current issues in academe. Familiar faces will begin to appear as you continue on the conference circuit. Don't hesitate to submit your own proposals for presentations. It is a good way to share your scholarship and indicates your willingness to do outreach.

Initial interviews are also often conducted at professional meetings where recent job openings may be announced or posted in a conspicuous place at the registration table. As a graduate student, many of these conferences are available to you at substantially reduced fees, and you should take advantage of them for the professional content as well as the opportunity to meet representatives from the departments of other higher-education institutions.

Possible Employers

In teaching, the possible employers are well documented. There is no "hidden job market," and most schools advertise widely. We have identified resources that can provide the names of potential employers.

Jobs Listed Online

A good way to begin reviewing job listings is to visit Academic Careers Online (academiccareers.com). Faculty positions at colleges, universities, and research institutes around the world are shown on this site. And if you use your favorite search engine and enter the keywords "college teaching jobs," you'll find a variety of sites listed.

Directories
Some resources that can be used to identify schools if you are considering teaching psychology include *Peterson's Two-Year Colleges, Peterson's Four-Year Colleges, Peterson's Guide to Graduate and Professional Programs*, and *The College Board Index of Majors and Graduate Degrees*. Peterson's website (peter sons.com) allows you to sort schools by specific majors offered, including psychology.

Psychology Department Postings
Sometimes when a hiring institution is seeking to fill a position under pressures of time, they will send notices of position openings to every school offering a program in psychology. Be sure to find out where the psychology department posts these notices at your school. Often you'll find them on a bulletin board near the department chair's office.

Professional Associations
Review carefully the list of professional associations for teachers of psychology that ends this chapter. Any activities that the association undertakes to assist its members in finding employment are shown.

Possible Job Titles

Job titles for positions relating to teaching and research in psychology will be fairly standard: teacher or researcher. Position descriptions will list areas of educational and research specialization required for the position. In both teaching and research, a specialization can be developed in one of the following subfields:

Clinical psychology
Community psychology
Counseling psychology
Developmental psychology
Educational psychology
Environmental psychology
Engineering psychology

Experimental psychology
Family psychology
Forensic psychology
Health psychology
Industrial and organizational psychology
Neuropsychology and psychobiology
Psychology and law, and forensic psychology
Psychology of aging
Psychology of women
Psychometrics and quantitative psychology
School psychology
Social psychology
Sports psychology

Related Occupations

If you've earned a master's degree or Ph.D. in psychology, you have developed an extensive knowledge and skill base that would be welcome in many other employment settings. Advanced academic work in psychology is perceived as valuable because it is highly transferable. In addition to your degree work, you would want to be able to satisfy the employer's demand for excellent skills in both verbal and written communications. Your well-developed research skills will be difficult for a commercial employer to assess unless you take the time to learn about their research needs and how you might be able to use your skills in their environment. Consider the following job titles as a beginning list and investigate these and other positions that draw on the skill base you know you possess.

Business manager
Consultant
Health professional
Human resources professional
Policy analyst
Public affairs specialist
Researcher
Therapist
Trainer
Writer

Professional Associations

The primary information resource for someone considering a career in teaching psychology at the college or university level is the American Psychological Association. Students are eligible to join at reduced rates, and by doing so they can begin the ever-important tasks of networking and gaining an insight on working as a professional in this field. Review the other associations to see if they also can assist in your job search.

American Psychological Association
750 First St. NE
Washington, DC 20002
apa.org
Members/Purpose: Scientific and professional society of psychologists with students participating as affiliates; advances psychology as a science, a profession, and a means of promoting human welfare; maintains fifty-three divisions
Training: Maintains an educational and training board
Journals/Publications: Visit website to review the APA's many publications
Job Listings: Career information and classified ads are available online

Association for the Advancement of Psychology
P.O. Box 38129
Colorado Springs, CO 80937
aapnet.org
Members/Purpose: Offers regular, organization, and student memberships; promotes human welfare through the advancement of the profession and science of psychology
Journals/Publications: *Advance* newsletter

Association of State and Provincial Psychology Boards
P.O. Box 241245
Montgomery, AL 36124
asppb.org
Members/Purpose: Alliance of state, provincial, and territorial agencies responsible for the licensure and certification of psychologists throughout the United States and Canada
Training: Publishes preparatory materials, validity studies, and guidelines
Journals/Publications: *ASPPB Newsletter*; *Handbook of Licensing and Certification Requirements*

International Council of Psychologists
c/o Dr. Kay C. Greene, Secretary General
4701 Willard Ave., Suite 1621
Chevy Chase, MD 20815-4630
members.tripod.com/icpsych
Members/Purpose: Psychologists and individuals professionally active in
  fields allied to psychology; advances psychology and furthers the
  application of its scientific findings
Training: Hosts annual convention
Journals/Publications: *World Psychology*; *International Psychologist*

National Education Association
1201 16th St. NW
Washington, DC 20036
nea.org
Members/Purpose: Professional organization and union of elementary and
  secondary school teachers, college and university professors,
  administrators, principals, counselors, and others concerned with
  education
Journals/Publications: *NEA Today*; *Higher Education Advocate*; *NEA
  Almanac of Higher Education*

Psi Chi, the National Honor Society in Psychology
P.O. Box 709
Chattanooga, TN 37403
psichi.org
Members/Purpose: National honor society in psychology
Journals/Publications: *Eye on Psi Chi*; *Psi Chi* newsletter

Additional Resources

ABI/Inform on Disk
UMI-Data Courier, Inc
300 N. Zeeb Rd.
P.O. Box 1346
Ann Arbor, MI 48106
umi.com

Alternatives to the Peace Corps: A Directory of Global Volunteer Opportunities
Food First
398 60th St.
Oakland, CA 94618
foodfirst.org

American Church List
InfoUSA
5711 S. 86th Circle
P.O. Box 27347
Omaha, NE 68127
americanchurchlists.com/ACL/index.aspx?bas_type=acl&bas_vendor=99889

America's Corporate Families
Dun & Bradstreet Information Services
899 Eaton Ave.
Bethlehem, PA 18025
dnb.com

America's Top Medical, Education, and Human Services Jobs
JIST Works, Inc
8902 Otis Ave.
Indianapolis, IN 46216
jist.com

Best's Insurance Reports
A.M. Best Co.
Ambest Rd.
Oldwick, NJ 08858
ambest.com

The Career Guide: Dun's Employment
   Opportunities Directory
Dun & Bradstreet Information Services
899 Eaton Ave.
Bethlehem, PA 18025
dnb.com

Career Opportunities in Education
Career Opportunities in Health Care
Career Opportunities in Politics,
   Government, and Activism
Facts on File
132 W. 31st St., 17th Floor
New York, NY 10001
factsonfile.com

Careers in Advertising
Careers in Communications
Careers in Computers
Careers in Health Care
Careers in Social and Rehabilitation Services
McGraw-Hill Companies
McGraw-Hill, Inc.
2 Penn Plaza
New York, NY 10121-2298
books.mcgraw-hill.com/searchseries.php?series=careers

Catholic Almanac
Our Sunday Visitor,
    Publishing Div.
200 Noll Plaza
Huntington, IN 46750
osv.com

The Chronicle of Higher Education
1255 23rd St. NW, Suite 700
Washington, DC 20037
chronicle.com

Cities Ranked and Rated: More than 400
    Metropolitan Areas Evaluated in the
    U.S. and Canada
John Wiley & Sons
111 River St.
Hoboken, NJ 07030-5774
wiley.com

The College Board Book of Majors
College Board Publication
45 Columbus Ave.
New York, NY 10023
collegeboard.org

The Complete Mental Health Directory
Grey House Publishing
P.O. Box 860
Millerton, NY 12546
greyhouse.com

Credit Unions Online Job Center (online)
Sponsored by CommonBond
    Communications, Inc.
P.O. Box 51297
Albuquerque, NM 87181
creditunionsonline.com/jobcenter.php

Dialing for Jobs: Using the Phone in the Job Search (DVD or VHS)
JIST Works, Inc.
8902 Otis Ave.
Indianapolis, IN 46216
jist.com

Directory of American Firms Operating in Foreign Countries
Uniworld Business Publications
3 Clark Rd.
Millis, MA 02054
uniworldbp.com

Directory of Public School Systems in the United States
American Association for Employment in Education
3040 Riverside Dr., Suite 125
Columbus, Ohio 43221
aaee.org

DISCOVER Career Guidance and Information System
American College Testing
500 Act Dr.
P.O. Box 168
Iowa City, IA 52243
act.org/discover

DotOrgJobs (online)
Sponsored by onPhilanthropy
dotorgjobs.com/rt/dojhome

Dow Jones Careers
Dow Jones & Co., Inc.
1 World Financial Center
200 Liberty St.
New York, NY 10281
dowjones.com/Careers/Careers.htm

Dun & Bradstreet's Million Dollar Databases
Dun & Bradstreet Information Services
899 Eaton Ave.
Bethlehem, PA 18025
dnbmdd.com/mddi

Encyclopedia of Associations:
  National Organizations of the U.S.
Thomson Gale
27500 Drake Rd.
Farmington Hills, MI 48331
gale.com

Environmental Opportunities
Environmental Studies Depart.
Antioch/New England Graduate School
40 Avon St.
Keene, NH 03431
antiochne.edu/ES/eao/jobs.cfm

Federal Jobs Digest
Breakthrough Publications, Inc.
325 Pennsylvania Ave. SE
Washington DC 20003
jobsfed.com

Foundation Grants to Individuals Online
The Foundation Center
79 Fifth Ave.
New York, NY 10003
fdncenter.org

Government Job Finder
Planning/Communications
7215 Oak Ave.
River Forest, IL 60305
planningcommunications.com/jf/index.htm

Graduate Admissions Essays:
  Write Your Way into the
  Graduate School of Your Choice
Ten Speed Press
Celestial Arts
Tricycle Press
P.O. Box 7123
Berkeley, CA 94707
tenspeedpress.com

Graduate Management Admission Test
Graduate Management Admission Council
1600 Tysons Blvd, Suite 1400
McLean, VA 22102
gmac.com/gmac/default.htm

Graduate Record Examinations
Graduate Record Examinations Board
Educational Testing Services
P.O. Box 6000
Princeton, NJ 08541
gre.org

Guide to America's Federal Jobs
JIST Works, Inc.
8902 Otis Ave.
Indianapolis, IN 46216
jist.com

The Handbook of Private Schools
Porter Sargent Publishers, Inc.
11 Beacon St., Suite 1400
Boston MA 02108
portersargent.com

Harrington-O'Shea Career
    Decision-Making System
American Guidance Service
4201 Woodland Rd.
Circle Pines, MN 55014
agsnet.com

Harvard Gazette
Harvard News Office
1060 Holyoke Center
1350 Massachusetts Ave.
Cambridge, MA 02138
hno.harvard.edu/gazette

Hoover's Handbook of American Business
Hoover's Inc.
5800 Airport Blvd.
Austin, TX 78752
hoovers.com/global/books/index.xhtml

How to Prepare Your Curriculum Vitae
McGraw-Hill Companies
McGraw-Hill, Inc.
2 Penn Plaza
New York, NY 10121-2298
books.mcgraw-hill.com/searchseries.php?series=careers

Infotrac CD-ROM Business & Index
Thomson Gale
27500 Drake Rd.
Farmington Hills, MI 48331
gale.com

Internships 2005
Peterson's Guide
Princeton Pike Corporate Ctr.
2000 Lenox Dr.
P.O. Box 67005
Lawrenceville, NJ 08648
petersons.com

JobFinder (online)
JCC Association of North America
15 E. 26th St.
New York, NY 10010-1579
jccworks.com

Jobs at Nonprofits Career Site (online)
Sponsored by Blackbaud
2000 Daniel Island Dr,
Charleston, SC 29492-7541
jobsatnonprofits.com

Medical and Health Information Directory
Thomson Gale
27500 Drake Rd.
Farmington Hills, MI 48331
gale.com

Myers-Briggs Type Indicator
CPP, Inc.
1055 Joaquin Rd., Suite 200
Mountain View, CA 94043
cpp.com/products/mbti/index.asp

The National Directory of Children, Youth, & Families Services
The National Directory of CYF Services
2795 E. Cottonwood Pkwy, Suite 140
Salt Lake City, UT 84121
childrenyouthfamilydir.com

The National JobBank 2006
Advanced Educational Products, Inc.
2495 Main St., Suite 230
Buffalo, NY 14214
aepbooks.com/Adams.html

National Trade and Professional Associations of the United States
Columbia Books Inc.
1825 Connecticut Ave. NW, Suite 625
Washington, DC 20009
columbiabooks.com

NationJob, Inc. (online)
601 SW 9th St., Suites J & K
Des Moines, IA 50309
nationjob.com

NICHCY State Resources
National Dissemination Center for Children with Disabilities
P.O. Box 1492
Washington, DC 20013
nichcy.org/states.htm

Occupational Outlook Handbook
U.S. Department of Labor
Bureau of Labor Statistics
Frances Perkins Building
200 Constitution Ave. NW
Washington, DC 20210
bls.gov/oco/home.htm

O'Dwyer's Directory of Public Relations Firms
J.R. O'Dwyer Co., Inc
271 Madison Ave., Suite 600
New York, NY 10016
odwyerpr.com

The 101 Toughest Interview Questions . . .
  and Answers That Win the Job!
JIST Works, Inc.
8902 Otis Ave.
Indianapolis, IN 46216
jist.com

O*NET Dictionary of Occupational Titles
JIST Works, Inc
8902 Otis Ave.
Indianapolis, IN 46216
http://online.onetcenter.org

Opportunities in Allied Health Careers
Opportunities in Gerontology and
  Aging Services Careers
Opportunities in Government Careers
Opportunities in Health and Medical Careers
Opportunities in Law Enforcement and
  Criminal Justice Careers
Opportunities in Occupational Therapy Careers
McGraw-Hill Companies
McGraw-Hill, Inc.
2 Penn Plaza
New York, NY 10121-2298
books.mcgraw-hill.com/searchseries.php?series=careers

Patterson's American Education
Patterson's Elementary Education
Educational Directories Unlimited, Inc.
University Technology Park II
1350 Edgmont Ave., Suite 1100
Chester, PA 19013
edudirectories.com

Peterson's Two-Year Colleges
Peterson's Four-Year Colleges
Peterson's
Princeton Pike Corporate Ctr.
2000 Lenox Dr.
P.O. Box 67005
Lawrenceville, NJ 08648
petersons.com

Security Dealers of North America
Standard and Poor's Corp.
55 Water St.
New York, NY 10041
standardandpoors.com

Skills Identification: Discovering Your Skills (DVD & VHS)
JIST Works, Inc.
8902 Otis Ave.
Indianapolis, IN 46216
jist.com

Standard and Poor's Register of Corporations
Standard and Poor's Corp.
55 Water St.
New York, NY 10041
standardandpoors.com

Strong Interest Inventory
CPP, Inc.
1055 Joaquin Rd., Suite 200
Mountain View, CA 94043
cpp.com/products/strong/index.asp

World Chamber of Commerce Directory
P.O. Box 1029
Loveland, CO 80539
wliinc2.com/secured/COFC/orderform.htm

Yearbook of American and Canadian Churches
National Council of Churches in the USA
110 Maryland Ave. NE
Washington, DC 20002
electronicchurch.org

Y National Vacancy List (online)
YMCA of the USA
101 N. Wacker Dr.
Chicago, IL 60606
ymca.net/employment/ymca_recruiting/jobright.htm

Index